IN THE TURKEY WOODS

Books by Jerome B. Robinson

Hunt Close
Training the Hunting Retriever
In the Turkey Woods

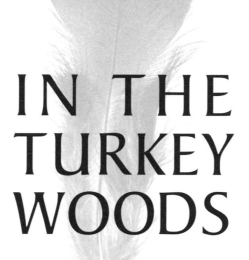

IN THE
TURKEY
WOODS

JEROME B. ROBINSON

THE LYONS PRESS

Printed in the United States of America

10 9 8 7 6 5 4 3 2

Design by Joel Friedlander, Marin Bookworks

Library of Congress Cataloging-in-Publication Data
    Robinson, Jerome B.
        In the turkey woods / Jerome B. Robinson.
                p.   cm.
        Includes index.
        ISBN 1-55821-695-2
        1. Turkey hunting.   I. Title.
    SK325.T8R635   1998
    799.2'4645—dc21   98-4725
                                        CIP

TABLE OF CONTENTS

ACKNOWLEDGMENTS

I am indebted to the following list of wild turkey specialists who graciously offered their time and expert knowledge, and to the editors of *Field & Stream* and *Sports Afield* who, year after year, sent me into the turkey woods to gather much of the information now collected in this book for articles published in those magazines.

Jamie Adams, Bushnell, Florida
Dave Berkeley, Bossier City, Louisiana
Doug Blodgett, Montpelier, Vermont
Rufus Brown, Gainesville, Georgia
Tad Brown, Columbia, Missouri
Don Carter, Gainesville, Georgia
Jim Clay, Winchester, Virginia
Sonny Conner, Eustis, Florida
John Cooper, Pierre, South Dakota
Jack Crockford, Chamblee, Georgia
John and Pauline Doty, Sedan, Kansas
Marc Drury, Columbia. Missouri
Terry Drury, Bloomsdale, Missouri
Mike Emberson, Bartlesville, Oklahoma
Ronnie Foy, Canton, Mississippi
John Hauer, Piedmont, South Dakota
Lon Lemmon, Fort Robinson, Nebraska
Richard McMullin, Bodcau WMA, Louisiana
Mike Morton, El Dorado, Arkansas
Roger Morton, El Dorado, Arkansas
Danny Pierce, Reydon, Oklahoma
Marc Scroggins, Oklahoma City, Oklahoma
Don Shipp, Clinton, Arkansas
Steve Stoltz, St. Louis, Missouri

Rex Suiter, Warsaw, Missouri
Ted Walski, Langdon, New Hampshire
John Williams, Kirksville, Missouri

INTRODUCTION

For the past 30 years, first as a writer for *Sports Afield* and more recently as a *Field & Stream* regular, it has been my frequent assignment to work with men who make their livings studying and pursuing wild turkeys. My goal is to find out what they know and what they do differently that brings them such success.

These men are turkey-hunting guides, championship turkey callers, turkey-call and -decoy manufacturers, biologists, documentary filmmakers, and just plain hunters who have special knowledge about wild turkeys. Each one spends more time in the turkey woods each season than many of us do in a lifetime; together they have acquired more firsthand knowledge of wild turkey behavior, motivation, and response than the rest of us would ever have figured out.

In these chapters you will learn how some of the most successful turkey hunters know how and when to use particular calls and sounds. You'll learn how to set decoys in the most productive manner, and you'll become convinced that the wise use of decoys conserves turkeys by drastically reducing crippling losses. I'll show you how to build your own turkey calls and give you some revolutionary information about important sounds turkeys make that humans cannot hear.

As we roll through the ranges of the Eastern, Osceola, Rio Grande, and Merriam wild turkey subspecies, hunting in states from northern New England to Florida, out through the Midwest to Texas, Nebraska, and South Dakota and back through Missouri and Virginia, you will pick up a load of useful turkey-hunting information from some of the best-educated experts in the turkey woods.

1

DAYBREAK
IN THE
TURKEY WOODS

It's not the shot that is the best part of turkey hunting. It's the luxury of being able to sit in absolute silence for long periods of time, simply observing the natural events as a new day begins in the forest.

As turkey hunters we spend a lot more time not hearing turkeys than we do hearing them, and a lot more time not seeing turkeys than seeing them. Still, each time we go turkey hunting we have an absolutely perfect opportunity to put all other cares aside while we become totally absorbed in nature's grand display.

One of the strangest places in which I have ever greeted a new day was the edge of a tropical swamp in central Florida. I was hunting Osceola turkeys with Jamie Adams near Bushnell.

About an hour before daylight Jamie dropped me off near some old cow pens in the center of a big cattle ranch, a mile or so off the

A lone gobbler roosts high in the tallest tree around so that his gobbling can be heard for the maximum distance, attracting hens from near and far.

road. I was to walk half a mile farther to a little field next to a vast swamp where Jamie thought a gobbler was likely to show up after dawn.

"Walk slow and take care you don't sit down on a snake or a fire-ant hill," he warned, then drove away.

I stood for a moment listening to the night sounds. A full moon and bright stars shone overhead, but ground fog obscured my surroundings. I could make out the dark shapes of live oaks bearded with Spanish moss; in a space between them the Hale-Bopp comet was a misty greenish blur.

I started down the trail but had gone only a short distance toward a barway when a dark shape loomed in the swirling mist, blocking my way. A few steps more brought me up short. The drooping ears and humped back told me it was a Brahma. I could see the bulge of the udder so at least it was a cow, not a bull, though I wasn't sure her gender made her any safer.

I waved my arms at the animal and made a whooshing sound intending to drive her away. The cow was not impressed. She lowered her head and emitted a deep bellow.

"Probably has a new calf," I thought. "Probably gonna kill you," my subconscious replied.

I gathered some chunks of limestone and pelted the cow with them. She backed off, allowing me through the gateway—but as I walked away quickly alongside a four-board fence, she came after me again in silent pursuit.

"If she gets too close I'll just roll under the fence," I thought. There was enough space beneath the bottom board for me to roll through. Then the cow rushed up to me and I hit the ground and rolled—and I was stopped by a woven wire fence stretched tight on the back of the fence posts.

This was a moment of definite terror. Then the cow stopped her charge, wheeled around, and trotted away, satisfied that she had dominated the situation. I got up and continued down the dim path beneath the moss-hung oaks into the darkness at the edge of the swamp.

The sounds that emanate from a tropical swamp at dawn on a warm spring morning are horrendous—like all the creatures of Hell are out there trying to strangle each other. Bull alligators bellow and slosh the water, herons scream their raucous chants, wild hogs squeal and grunt, raccoons squall, owls hoot, and, to top things off, wild turkeys yelp and gobble and cackle as they fly down.

I sat down in awe. A new day broke in a world where it seemed I was the only human and the concept of civilization was very remote.

When the sky brightened and a warm sun rose, the sounds mellowed and grew less menacing. The horrible squawks and screams that had unnerved me in the darkness I now could see were made by stately sandhill cranes that danced on the open prairies in graceful courtship rituals; the squealing of the wild hogs now seemed just like normal farm sounds. The bull alligators lay peacefully in the sun, and the Brahma cattle that shuffled into my corner of the pasture were just cows and calves. They no longer suggested the fearsome beast that had confronted me in the darkness and the swirling mists a couple of hours before.

"It's easier to hide from a deer than it is to hide from a cow," Sonny Conner had told me, and he was right. Within a few minutes cows and calves completely encircled my turkey decoys, and a rough-looking, sandy-colored critter stood 10 feet from my blind, staring at me and snuffling.

When the bunch left I was alone. No turkeys answered my calls that morning, but I had had a full and memorable experience nonetheless.

Nor shall I forget the first morning I went out to listen for turkeys in the Georgia mountains. It was cold. Frost whitened the grass as I set out across the meadow from our cabin, heading for a steep hill that would make a good listening spot.

I was halfway across the meadow when a sound from a cattle feeder startled me. I dipped into my pocket for a flashlight, thinking, "deer." But the eyes that shone in my beam were red, and the hulk that surrounded them was huge and black. It was a bear, and not just your everyday 200-pounder.

This bear had a head like a bushel basket. Fat rolled beneath his glistening hide as he walked, not ran, away from me, bound for the same steep hillside trail that I had planned to climb. Undoubtedly he was the bear that had been described to us the night before. He had been seen regularly in this remote mountain valley and exhibited little fear of man. Those who had seen him said he was surely a 500-pounder.

I watched the big bear shamble away and take the uphill trail. I knew I should follow him and not let his presence intimidate me. There were bears all over these hills, after all. But man, he was *big*.

As he disappeared into the predawn murk I decided to go up the creek instead. Eventually I sat in a place where the creek noise made it impossible to hear distant turkeys, and I jumped at every nearby sound. I felt foolish for letting the bear rattle me but, at the same time, grateful for having seen the big animal up close. When the sun rose and the redbirds began to sing, my encounter with the bear seemed marvelous. I was grateful that the mountains still harbored such a great beast and that he had not felt threatened by my appearance.

Still, the mornings I dwell on in my dreams are those filled with turkey sounds.

Like the time in Texas when I set my decoys in a little strip of trees at the edge of a big open pasture from which a long timbered draw ran away to the south. I have never heard so many gobblers greet the day as there were that morning.

For 15 minutes before dawn turkeys gobbled in waves of staccato sound that rippled over the Texas prairie and evoked still more gobbling. I have no idea how many turkeys there were in that draw, but it was clearly packed, and every gobbler wanted to be heard.

I could hear the flapping as hens flew down; a few minutes later all of the gobbling stopped as breeding activity began. Suddenly the morning was as still as a tomb.

An hour later, when a gobbler answered my call, the sound seemed out of place. When he answered again a few moments later from half the distance it seemed a miracle: With all those turkeys around he had singled out my imperfect sounds and was coming to me. And when he finally came mincing through the trees all puffed up and blue in the face, the sun lit up his red wattles, and the copper and bronze lights in his body feathers were magnificent. I can still see his tail fanned full, turning this way and that in the early-morning sunlight as he sought the hen he had heard calling from where I sat.

Then I remember all the mornings when turkey sounds filled the air at dawn, yet nothing I could say or do brought a turkey my way. Rather than feeling disappointed I end such mornings feeling immensely rich; I know that the woods are full of turkeys and that they will be there for me to hunt again another day.

2

USING
TURKEY
DECOYS

" I used to hunt with an ole boy who had a turkey decoy he whittled outa some kinda hard plastic foam his wife's new washin' machine came packed in. He'd lug that thing around, clunkin' and bangin' through the woods, always swearin' about what a load it was, but you know, it worked. He shot turkeys, and when he shot 'em they were close—15 or 20 yards. Didn't matter what kinda gun he shot or how tight it was choked. Man, he flat killed 'em dead with one shot every time."

Ronnie Foy was telling the story. He runs Foy's Guiding Service in Canton, Mississippi (601-859-2300), and over the years his clients have scored an outstanding 86 percent success rate on longbeards (no jake shooting permitted). He uses decoys religiously.

"One day I come home from the store with one of these new collapsible decoys and showed it to that ole boy," Ronnie continued. "He like to had a fit.

"'Why, you can roll that thing up and carry it in your over-hauls,' he crowed. 'No noise, not catchin' on ever' damn thing. I got to git me one o' them right quick.'

"We jumped in his truck and headed back to the store. He had his ole decoy in the back," Ronnie went on. "'You sure they got more o' them decoys in that store?' he kept askin' me.

"'They got a whole pile of 'em,' I told him.

"We was just then crossin' a bridge," Ronnie recalled. "That ole boy slammed on his brakes and got out. He pulled his ole decoy out of the truck and threw it in the river.

Turkey decoys take the approaching gobbler's eye off the spot that he hears the calls coming from and help to pull him within absolute killing range—if your calling is good and you sit still.

"'Then that's the end o' that damn thing,' he said. 'My life's fixin' to change.'"

The lives of many turkey hunters have changed recently as new, collapsible, very realistic turkey decoys have swept the marketplace, enabling hunters to conveniently carry decoys that give gobblers something to look at when they come to a hunter's call.

A decoy takes the turkey's eye off the spot that he heard the call coming from. Instead of looking right at you the turkey comes in focused on the decoy, and you can let him approach to within very close range, take careful aim, and kill him with a single shot. In this way decoys save a lot of turkeys from being crippled by hunters who would otherwise take long shots, hoping to get lucky, on birds that hang up and won't come into absolute killing range.

As the use of turkey decoys becomes more popular every year (all states but Alabama now permit them) hunters are finding that there are right ways and not-so-right ways to set them. Also, certain types of decoys can do more harm than good in some situations.

Dave Berkley, founder of the outstanding Feather-Flex line of turkey decoys, has researched how turkeys respond to decoys and gives very clear advice on how decoys should be used.

"For most situations I use one little standing jake and two hen decoys, and I set them with three things in mind," he explains. "First, decoys only work if they can be seen, so you want to set them in an open spot (along the edge of a field or in a forest opening) where a gobbler will see them from a good distance.

"Second, it's very important to set the jake decoy no more than 20 yards from where the shooter will sit, and to place the shooter where he will have a clear view and a comfortable shot at the jake decoy, because you can just about guarantee that if a gobbler comes in he will go to the jake decoy first.

"Third, you want to be able to see clearly beyond the decoys so that if some foolish hunter mistakes them for real turkeys and tries to

Set the decoys in an open place where they can be seen from a long distance.

Gobblers usually go to the little standing jake decoy first, so place it where you will have a comfortable shot, about 20 yards away.

stalk them, you'll see him and can call out to him before he gets ready to shoot."

THE IMPORTANCE OF THE JAKE DECOY

"The jake is your most important decoy," Dave insists. "It's the jake, more than the hen, decoy that can make the gobbler take those extra steps that bring him into absolute killing range."

The small standing jake, identifiable from a long distance by his red wattles, jutting immature beard, and nonaggressive posture, is not seen as a threat by most mature longbeards. In fact most mature male gobblers immediately recognize that they can whip a little single jake and come in with the intention of driving the little jake away.

"Look at it like this," Dave explains. "In nature the gobbler responds to a hen call and moves to a position where the hen can see him strut and hear him drumming. At that point the gobbler stops and hangs up; the hen is supposed to run to him. As hunters we are

The little standing jake decoy is in a nonaggressive pose. Most gobblers are not afraid to challenge it and will try to drive it off.

Hen decoys give an approaching gobbler something to look at that explains your calling, but the gobbler may hang up out of range and demand that the hen go to him. When a little standing jake decoy is used in combination with a hen decoy, however, most gobblers will come all the way in and attempt to drive the jake away.

opposing nature by demanding that the gobbler come all the way to the hen instead of waiting for the hen to go to him.

"That's where the jake decoy comes into play," Dave continues. "When a gobbler sees a young jake already with the hen, his jealousy is aroused, and he will come all the way in to drive the little jake away. That's why the gobbler always goes to the jake decoy first, and why the jake decoy should be placed exactly where the hunter wants to shoot."

The only time a gobbler may initially head toward a decoy other than the jake is when you use an orange-headed safety decoy. Three years ago Feather-Flex, Inc. (manufacturer of the largest market share of turkey decoys), introduced the first safety decoy, an orange-headed hen whose presence in a decoy set warns interloping hunters that they are looking at decoys, not live targets. (See chapter 4 for more information on the safety decoy.)

Gobblers are unlikely to come all the way to a lone hen decoy, but if you add a nonaggressive little standing jake decoy (right), they will often come all the way in to drive the jake off. Place the jake no more than 20 yards away, in a comfortable shooting position.

Recently several decoy manufacturers have introduced jake decoys in more aggressive poses—half strut and full strut. In specific situations these decoys can be very effective, but they are not intended to be used all the time. In fact jake decoys in these aggressive poses will cause less aggressive gobblers to shy away.

"You've got to know what kind of gobbler you're working on," says Dave. "Sometimes you run into an old dominant gobbler that is so sure of himself that he just stands out in the middle of a big open field and gobbles and struts and demands that the hens go to him. You can't call him. He plain refuses to take a step toward a hen call. That's the kind of bird that is impossible to kill according to common methods. Yet he may succumb to a jake decoy in an aggressive pose.

The half-strut decoy is in a very menacing pose, which indicates that he is ready to defend his territory. This decoy will scare off gobblers that don't want a fight. Use it only on dominant gobblers that ignore the little standing jake decoy.

The full-strut decoy is also in an aggressive pose that will frighten many gobblers away. Again, use it only on dominant gobblers that ignore the little standing jake decoy.

"When I get on a bird like that I go in early and put a strutting jake decoy within sight of where the old bird likes to strut, and I surround it with hen decoys. Give the illusion that there is a brash youngster in the place that has stolen the old bird's hens. When the old gobbler gets in position I'll give a few hen calls to make him look at the decoys, then a short high-pitched gobble to make him mad, and then let nature take over. If he's going to come that old bird will come directly, on the run, right to that jake decoy."

Choosing which decoy to use depends a lot upon your knowledge of the turkey you're hunting. There are three basic types of male turkeys roaming the woods in the spring. To decoy them effectively you must understand their differences.

JAKES

The spring turkey woods are occupied by roaming bands of jakes—year-old males with strong mating urges but inferior body size. They can be distinguished from mature males by their smaller size, their shorter beards, and the longer length of the center feathers in their tail fans.

Jakes are easily drawn to hen calls but may be wary about approaching close until they are assured that no larger gobbler is present and likely to attack them. If they are in groups, however, their machismo increases; they may abandon discretion and storm a decoy set with great bravado.

Like teenage hoodlums, they sometimes gang up on mature single gobblers and attack them—which is why you should never put out more than one little jake decoy. Two or more little jakes might be seen as a threatening gang, and many older gobblers will steer clear of them.

On the other hand, the jake gangs themselves are very susceptible to single nonaggressive little jake decoys. When they spot a little jake decoy standing innocently beside a hen decoy jake gangs go on the warpath. They come trotting in all puffed up in strutting positions, gobbling simultaneously with such a clamor that you'd think a 50-pound turkey was about to enter the scene.

Jakes are great. They do all the classic things that gobblers are supposed to do, and they often come to calls and decoys with complete abandon, soothing the bruised pride of hunters who have had little luck with older birds.

Some hunters prefer not to shoot jakes. They argue that "this year's jake is next year's trophy longbeard." Yet jakes are legal game and superior table fare. For the good of a local turkey population, though, it would probably be best to shoot only jakes and birds of three years or more, saving the two-year-olds (which are proved survivors) to be next year's most active breeders.

Jakes respond best to simple decoy sets of one or two hens and are usually excited by the addition of a single small jake decoy in a nonaggressive pose.

SUBDOMINANT GOBBLERS

In every turkey population the largest number of gobblers are subdominant birds that gobble a lot and grow big and fat, but rarely fight and breed few hens. They may tag along with a dominant breeding gobbler, watching him score but never challenging his dominance, or they may wander alone through the woods quietly, trying to find an occasional hen and breeding her without attracting the attention (and wrath) of the dominant gobbler.

Two hen decoys and a single little standing jake decoy is usually the most effective set for subdominant gobblers. If a gobbler approaches but refuses to come in to such a set, however, Dave Berkley marks that individual as extra shy and unwilling to confront even a nonaggressive little standing jake. The next time Dave goes after that bird he won't put out the jake decoy, and he may use only one hen decoy.

"There are some gobblers whose standing is so low in the pecking order that they tend to avoid any situation that seems to suggest confrontation," Dave explains. "These birds can be of any age and are often very large, since they do not waste energy fighting and rarely breed.

"This bird has indicated by coming to your calls the first time that he is susceptible to calling and wants to have the opportunity to breed, but he is not willing to confront other male turkeys.

"What he wants is a single hen with no other turkeys around. Put the hen where he can see that it's alone and then call sparingly. Once you know that he's approaching (he may cluck but probably won't gobble), sit still and position yourself so that you can shoot when he circles the spot where he hears the calls coming from, for he will probably circle to make sure no other turkeys are present before he approaches the hen decoy.

"When you know that you're working a particularly shy bird you want to keep your eyes peeled, because that kind usually sneaks in without saying a thing," Dave warns.

THE DOMINANT GOBBLER

This is the bird that rules the roost. Often he is not the heaviest gobbler around, but he is the fastest and the most fierce. The dominant gobbler is the bird least likely to come to hen calls or hen decoys. He is used to having hens go to him, so he'll refuse to go to them unless he's challenged by the presence of an aggressive jake that he perceives to be intruding in his territory and stealing the attention of his hens.

He often roosts alone and will not fly down until several hens have gathered under his roosting tree and demonstrated a willingness to breed. When he does fly down he goes directly to his hens and cannot be called away from them. He becomes vulnerable, however, when he moves to his midmorning strut zone.

"This is the bird you need to challenge. He won't come to a hen decoy or a nonaggressive little standing jake decoy, but he may not be able to stand the sight of another gobbler strutting with hens. In this case an aggressive strutting decoy surrounded by hen decoys may prove intolerable," says Dave.

KNOW YOUR BIRDS

Ronnie Foy spends a great deal of time studying turkeys on the many thousands of acres he controls. "Knowin' your birds is the name of the game," he insists. "If I know where birds are gonna go on their way from the roost to their feedin' spots I can set up in a place I know the birds will come sometime that day. I think that's

Place decoys in an open place where they can be seen from a distance and where any air movement will cause them to turn with lifelike motion.

more important than knowin' which tree a gobbler roosted in. When I know where the birds are gonna go I can set my decoys in a place where they're gonna be seen. Then I just call a little bit from time to time. Gobblers are much more likely to go to calls they hear comin' from spots where they expect turkeys to be."

Movement also contributes to the effectiveness of turkey decoys. "You want to rig your decoys so they move with the slightest breath of air," says Ronnie. "I like the Feather-Flex decoys that stand on a spindle that goes up through the body and fits in a grommet at the top of the back. They'll turn with the air currents and add life to the set."

"'Course, you don't want 'em to move so much that they seem unnatural. When it's real windy I push strong twigs into the ground on both sides of the decoy's tail to keep it from spinnin' around," Ronnie adds.

Decoys can be used as range markers, too. "I usually set one hen at 30 yards as a range marker and tell my hunters not to shoot until the gobbler's come closer than that hen. Then I tell them to let him come as close as he will—no use shootin' at 30 yards if he's gonna come all the way to the jake that's placed at 20 yards," Ronnie advises.

Ronnie Foy sets his jake decoy facing the hunter's position because, he says, most times a gobbler will confront the jake decoy head to head, with its tail fan blocking its view of the hunter.

"When he spreads his fan and turns it toward you, you raise your gun; next time he sleeks and his head is clear, you shoot," Ronnie says. "Or you can raise your gun slowly when his head goes behind somethin' as he comes in. Then keep your bead on his wattles as he comes into killin' range and shoot when you have a clear view of his head and neck."

All this being said, it's important to understand that decoys do not work every time, on every bird. They are a tool—just like a turkey call—that can appreciably increase your chances of success when used properly. But there are times when gobblers ignore decoys and times when some birds even become shy of them.

For safety when using decoys, sit with your back against an object that's wider than your shoulders and taller than your head so that you can't be shot from behind. Call out if you see a hunter stalking your decoys.

"Location is probably the most important factor," says Ronnie Foy. "You've gotta be where a turkey wants to be. That's why knowin' your birds is so important."

SETTING DECOYS SAFELY

When used properly turkey decoys actually make turkey hunting safer.

Always sit with your back against an object wider than your shoulders and higher than your head. That way you can't be shot from behind.

Next, set your decoys where you can see over them for a long distance. If you spot another hunter coming into that line of fire holler, "Don't shoot! These are decoys." Don't move or wave your hands—your movement might be mistaken for a turkey's. Just shout until the other hunter recognizes what he's hearing.

Don't worry about spooking turkeys by shouting. The moving

hunter will already have spooked any that might have been out there.

With your backside blocked and a good view out over your decoys, you have covered the dangerous lines of fire. If some crazed hunter creeps in and takes a potshot at your decoys from any other angle he may hit the decoys, but he can't hit you.

Turkey-hunting accidents occur when an overexcited hunter hears a turkey calling and is drawn to the sound. He becomes convinced that there's a turkey just ahead. Suddenly he sees movement, shoulders his gun, and fires.

In heavily hunted Missouri 152 turkey hunters have been accidentally shot in the past 10 years, but only one of those accidents involved a turkey decoy—a full-bodied, noncollapsible decoy that the hunter was carrying out of the woods when he was shot.

It's calling and movement, not decoys, that cause turkey-hunting accidents.

MORE ON DECOYS

DO TURKEYS GET DECOY-SHY?

Hunters sometimes see turkeys veer away from decoys and get the mistaken impression that the birds are "decoy-shy."

Instead it is much more likely that these turkeys are "turkey-shy."

During the height of the breeding season, when gobblers are following groups of hens, the hens in these groups all know each other and a certain pecking order has been established among them. Often these hen groups don't want competition from hens that they don't know, so they avoid them.

Thus when they see decoys and hear aggressive hen sounds coming from them, hens sometimes veer off and drift away, thinking that they're avoiding a conflict with strange turkeys. And if gobblers are traveling with a group of hens that takes such evasive action when it encounters strange turkeys, they usually go where the hens go and avoid the confrontation, too.

But it's not decoys they're avoiding, it's turkeys.

At other times some single gobblers act nervous and refuse to approach decoys closely. It's easy to assume that they don't like something about the decoys.

But consider this: Subdominant gobblers that have been hurt in fights with dominant gobblers are often wary of groups of turkeys because they fear that an unseen mature gobbler may be nearby, ready to come after them. These birds may avoid groups of decoys but will often come in to calls when only a single hen decoy is used.

Decoys also frequently get the blame for times when a turkey runs away. What actually scared the bird, though, was not the decoys but something else — a slight movement of the hunter or the flash of sunlight on a moving shotgun.

When a gobbler sees your decoys and then avoids them, ask yourself why. It's very unlikely that the bird was put off by the decoys; more likely he either saw you or just didn't want to join other turkeys for reasons of his own.

Remember, too, that most gobblers are less likely to come all the way to a single hen decoy. Nature says that the hen should go to the gobbler, so when you use a single hen decoy the gobbler may hang up within sight of it and display himself and drum and gobble, demanding that the decoy move to him.

When the hen decoy fails to approach him and the hens he has with him are drifting away, he may leave, too.

For this reason it is usually best to use a hen and a little non-aggressive standing jake decoy in combination. Most gobblers that come close but not all the way to a single hen decoy *will* come all the way in to drive the little jake away. Thus they'll present you with a shot within a few feet of the little jake decoy.

THE IMPORTANCE OF DECOY MOTION

Nothing makes a decoy more convincing to a turkey than motion. If the decoy moves when the turkey is looking at it, he is going to go to it.

Some hunters who use rigid decoys attach strings to them to make them move, but such arrangements are slow to set up, inconvenient to use, and likely to fail at crucial moments if the string snags on an obstruction or the hunter is seen as he jerks the string.

I use the same collapsible Feather-Flex foam decoys that Ronnie Foy uses (see chapter 2); they're so light that even faint air currents cause them to turn on their spindles in a very realistic manner.

When the air is still, however, I don't place the point of the spindle in its grommet; instead I set it to rest against the inside of the decoy at a point very close beside the grommet. This creates an almost friction-free arrangement and allows the decoy to turn on the spindle with only the faintest breath of air. I also enlarge the hole in the bottom of the decoy to allow the decoy to turn more freely on the spindle.

To avoid having a decoy spin on a windy day, I push a couple of foot-tall twigs into the ground about 6 inches on either side of the decoy's tail—just as Ronnie does. The twigs stop the decoy from turning too far and the resulting back-and-forth motion is very turkeylike.

I saw a good example of how important decoy motion is in the spring of 1997. I was hunting a thickly forested hill near my home in New Hampshire and had placed my decoys in the middle of a narrow logging road. Decoys, of course, must be placed where turkeys can see them, and this logging road was the only open place around.

I had heard no turkeys gobbling, so I was just setting up blind in an area I knew turkeys used frequently. At 5 A.M. I heard a distant answer to my calling. I replied with a series of loud cutts and then laid my box call in the leaves.

The next time I heard the turkey he was only about 100 yards away. He had come this far without gobbling, but now he sounded off with two or three loud announcements. This time I did not answer him. He knew where my earlier calls had come from, and I wanted him to hunt for me, not just stand out there gobbling invitations for the hen he had heard to join him.

When he gobbled again he had halved the distance between us and was now on the other side of a very thick spruce-fir thicket. He gobbled several times from that position and then began to circle to the left. The next time I heard him he was less than 50 yards away and still moving left.

I gave him three soft clucks to assure him that I had not moved, then put my call away again. He gobbled several times from his new position, but I didn't answer anymore. I was sure that he was committed and would next begin to hunt for me and discover the decoys.

A rise in the ground prevented me from seeing him, but now I heard the old bird drum from a position in thick growth maybe 30 yards out behind the decoys. At any second he would surely get to where he could see them. I heard him drum again.

Finally I spotted a slight movement; then I saw him. He had come out of the thicket and was standing motionless, long-necking the decoys. The air had been perfectly still and the decoys looked alarmingly lifeless. Live turkeys move and communicate with body language. I worried that the gobbler would hang up where he was, waiting for the hen decoy to move to him.

But just then a breath of air stirred. The soft new maple leaves overhead moved ever so slightly. And now the decoys moved. The air current was just enough to turn both decoys on their spindles about 45 degrees, first one and then the other.

When a breath of air caused the decoys to move, the gobbler popped into full strut and began his march straight toward the jake decoy.

The effect was like magic. As soon as the decoys moved the gobbler popped into full strut. He threw his chest out, his long beard sprouting and his magnificent tail fanned full. He drove his wing tips into the earth, he pulled in his chin, and his head went white. Now he began his march straight to the jake decoy in short bursts of three or four quick steps alternating with pauses in which he shivered all over and his head flashed red, white, and blue.

When I fired he was only inches from the jake decoy—so close that the edge of my pattern caught the decoy and put four holes in its head as well.

That was a grand three-year-old longbeard. He had acted a little leery of the decoys when they stood motionless for an unnatural length of time, but once they moved the game was over. He came in absolutely convinced that the jake decoy was a rival that had to be run off and I shot him at 18 yards—an absolutely lethal range with any shotgun.

Decoys are never a guarantee, but when they are rigged to move with turkeylike motion, the odds that a gobbler will come to them go way, way up.

BEWARE OF STRUTTING GOBBLER DECOYS

Recently sales of gobbler decoys in aggressive full-strut and half-strut positions have been going through the roof. Many hunters are buying them for the wrong reasons, though, and finding out too late that most of the time these specialty decoys don't work. In fact lots of times they not only don't draw turkeys in but actually scare gobblers away.

The gobbler-in-strut decoys are wonderfully realistic to look at, but they are made for the specific purpose of antagonizing those rare aggressive dominant gobblers that absolutely refuse to come to turkey calls. Unless you are hunting an individual bird that you know meets this description, never use a decoy that represents a gobbler in full-strut or half-strut position.

Before you choose a decoy you must understand this about turkey behavior: Long before the active breeding season begins male turkeys in large wintering flocks establish a pecking order. The bird that wins all the fights and can peck on every other bird in the flock is the dominant, or alpha, male. Every turkey in the vicinity recognizes him and respects his position. Other male turkeys either avoid the alpha male or are submissive in his presence.

These tough old dominant birds are the most active breeders. Hens seem to understand that the dominant bird is superior and will therefore respond to his summons when he gobbles or struts to attract them to him.

Sometimes these dominant gobblers are so sure of their allure that they don't even bother answering the calls of seductive hens. Instead they just go to a highly visible strutting zone and hang around for hours, strutting and displaying themselves. They never go to a hen—the hens always go to them.

No amount of calling will break such a bird out of his strut zone and cause him to come to you. You can show him hen decoys and even little jake decoys; he'll ignore them. Calling or decoying such a bird is almost impossible with normal decoys.

However, when you know where such a bird hangs out (often way out in an open field or large opening in the forest) *you have the single situation when a gobbler-in-strut decoy is called for:*

An aggressive dominant male turkey cannot abide the sight of a strange mature male displaying on his turf.

If you put a gobbler-in-strut decoy on the edge of the dominant bird's favored strutting field, surround it with a hen decoy or two, and then make a few hen calls or gobbler clucks to attract the dominant bird's eye and make him see the intruder, there's a good chance the old bird will come over to do battle with the intention of driving the stranger away.

There is really no other situation that calls for a gobbler-in-strut decoy. If you are hunting any gobbler farther down in the pecking order, the sight of a gobbler-in-strut decoy may cause him to drift away: The average gobbler is not looking for a fight once the active breeding season has begun.

Gobbler-in-strut decoys can also be dangerous, particularly in states where rifles are permitted for use on turkeys. They may draw fire from a hunter who mistakes them for the real thing.

Recognizing this possibility, Feather-Flex offers gobbler-in-strut decoys with hunter-safety orange heads, orange wing patches, and orange tail tips. These do not detract from their ability to raise the ire of a dominant gobbler but are effective in warning hunters that they are looking at a decoy, not a real bird.

"Trouble is, when hunters see a gobbler shy away from an orange-headed gobbler-in-strut decoy they often blame the failure on the orange color and never realize that it is the aggressive posture of the gobbler-in-strut decoy that drives average turkeys away, not the orange," notes Feather-Flex's Dave Berkley.

Dave worries that sales of gobbler-in-strut decoys are soaring for the wrong reasons. "Hunters like the looks of gobblers in strutting positions and don't realize that the aggressive postures will frighten most gobblers away," he says. "Then they get the mistaken impression that turkey decoys don't work when the real problem is that they are using the wrong type of decoy."

4

THE ORANGE-HEADED SAFETY DECOY

When the Feather-Flex decoy company introduced the blaze orange-headed "safety hen" turkey decoy in 1994, the company was defying conventional wisdom and flying in the face of the universally accepted theory that declares blaze orange a hex on successful turkey hunting.

Back then just about everyone believed that blaze orange on a turkey decoy would scare wild turkeys right out of the woods.

There was even a study completed by an eminent turkey biologist, who had hoped to determine that turkey hunters could use orange in some way to identify their locations without reducing their chances of success. To his disappointment his study indicated that orange markers caught the attention of approaching turkeys and spooked them.

"I read that study and immediately saw a hole in it," recalls Feather-Flex's Dave Berkley. "The man had tied an orange band around the tree he was sitting against and hoped that turkeys would disregard the orange and come to his calls anyway. Instead he found that the birds noticed the orange and were spooked.

"Now think about that for a minute," Dave continues. "The turkey is drawn in by the sounds of a seductive hen and comes in looking for her. Instead of seeing a hen, the turkey's attention is drawn to a bright orange banner at precisely the spot the hen sounds are coming from.

"The orange band draws the turkey's attention to the tree the man is sitting against. That just makes it more likely that the turkey will notice the unnatural shape of the man sitting against the tree. His caution lights will go on, and he is more apt to 'putt' and drift away."

Was it the orange that spooked the turkey? No. The orange merely drew the turkey's attention and made it easier for him to spot the hunter, Dave decided.

Dave figured that if he put the orange on the decoy instead of the hunter's hiding place, the turkey's attention would be drawn to the decoys and away from the hidden hunter's location. This would be an advantage to the hunter and would certainly add a degree of safety to turkey hunting: Any approaching hunter's eye would also be caught by the orange-headed decoy, and he would be less likely to mistake the decoys for live birds.

"I didn't know how turkeys would react to an orange-headed decoy, but anyone who has been around poultry knows that birds are curious about unnatural colors on other birds," Dave continues. "Put a drop of red on a chicken and what happens? The other birds are drawn to the unnatural color and they peck at it. Unless you separate the odd-colored chicken the rest of the flock will peck it to death."

Dave had a hunch that wild turkeys would react similarly to the sight of unnatural color on a turkey decoys—and he was absolutely right.

In subsequent field testing wild turkeys not only proved to be unafraid of the orange-headed decoy but were also frequently drawn to it first. When called into the visual range of decoys wild turkeys often went directly to the orange-headed decoy and ignored its natural-colored counterparts.

I first saw the orange-headed safety decoy on a hunt in Oklahoma with Dave Berkley and turkey-calling champion Mike Emberson in 1994 when the orange-headed decoys were still being field-tested.

The fluorescent orange on the safety decoy (left) draws the attention of approaching gobblers to the decoy set and takes the turkey's eye off the spot where the hunter is sitting. It does not spook gobblers. In fact, gobblers are often attracted to the orange-headed decoy and go to it first.

Dave Berkeley of Feather-Flex developed the orange-headed safety decoy to make using turkey decoys safer.

We had set the orange-headed hen decoy with a natural-colored hen decoy and a natural-colored jake decoy along the timbered edge of a big soybean field where two Rio Grande gobblers had been seen strutting the day before.

At dawn the gobblers answered our calls. When they flew down they landed within sight about 100 yards away. For a while they strutted and gobbled where they had landed, but when our decoys failed to run to them the two gobblers began marching our way in full strut.

If they noticed anything wrong with the orange-headed decoy they didn't show it. Instead both birds went into a menacing half-strut position and, passing within inches of the orange-headed hen decoy, went head to head with the jake decoy placed a few feet away. When I fired the dominant gobbler was poised for battle with the jake decoy, and the subdominant gobbler was standing within three feet of the orange-headed hen.

After that Dave and I drove to Missouri to hunt some land in the hill country that Tad Brown had told us held several big old Eastern gobblers.

We worked one vocal gobbler all morning. He answered every call but he was clearly with hens and unwilling to break away from them to come to us. When he finally drifted away we moved up to where he had been and found feathers and drag marks where he'd been strutting in a little forest opening above a creek.

"This is his strut zone," Dave declared. "He'll be back here tomorrow, but we'll be here first."

The next morning we were in the strut zone and had our decoys placed in a noticeable location before daylight. Dawn came, and we could hear distant gobbling, but no birds answered our calls. Dave decided to go after one of the distant birds, leaving me sitting over the decoys in the strut zone.

He hadn't been gone for more than 10 minutes when a gobbler sounded off about a quarter mile up the creek.

I answered with some insistent yelps, and he boomed right back at me. I yelped again, and he answered again. He seemed to be a little nearer. The next time he gobbled the bird had cut the distance between us in half. He was clearly coming in a hurry.

I didn't make a sound. As long as the bird was headed my way I wanted to let him come and not give him the idea that he could call me to him.

He gobbled again when he was 50 yards away across the creek behind me. I gave him back three soft clucks and went silent.

I heard the flutter of his wings as he crossed the creek. Then I could hear him spit and drum directly behind me. I fought the temptation to turn my head for a peek but rolled my eyes backward as far as I could. I tried to ignore the mosquito that chose this moment to begin a drilling operation on my nose.

Then I saw him. He was coming up on my right side, and he was in full strut. The pulmonic boom of his drumming sounded like a truck starting up in the distance. He was only 20 yards away, but he was on my off side, and I could not get my gun on him without turning.

I didn't have to worry, though. The bird had seen the decoys and was totally focused on them. In full strut, he minced his steps and closed in on the decoys. But rather than going to the jake decoy that I had placed 20 yards away in a clear and perfect shooting position, the gobbler went directly to the orange-headed safety decoy—which, from my position, was obscured behind a tree.

When he reached the orange-headed decoy the gobbler disappeared from my view. I could see only his tail feathers sticking out from behind the tree trunk. From the way his tail was bobbing up and down it appeared he was either going to attack the decoy or mount and try to breed it.

Then he turned so that his tail protruded from the other side of the tree. His body and head remained hidden, though.

Just then a puff of breeze blew through the woods and caused the jake decoy to turn on its spindle.

That was too much for the gobbler. He left the orange-headed decoy and strode across the opening in a menacing half-strut position to confront the jake.

When his head disappeared behind a tree I raised my gun, and when it reappeared I fired, dropping the big gobbler in his tracks three feet from the jake decoy and less than 20 yards from where I sat.

"He wasn't afraid of that orange-headed decoy, was he?" Dave Berkley demanded when he rejoined me.

"Hell, no," I said. "He wanted to breed it."

That was a 24½-pound gobbler with a 10½-inch beard and 1½-inch spurs—a prime four-year-old at the peak of his development—

and not only was he unafraid of the orange-headed decoy but he had gone to it first.

Since that hunt I have used the orange-headed safety decoy regularly and seen more than 50 turkeys come in to it. I have never witnessed any show of concern about the color. Turkeys either ignore it or are actually attracted to it.

On a number of occasions I have talked with other hunters who encountered my decoys as they slipped through the woods. They invariably say, "That orange-headed decoy was the first thing I saw, and I knew right away I was looking at decoys."

There is no question that it makes turkey hunting with decoys safer.

Some hunters fear that turkeys will learn to connect orange-headed decoys with danger, but Dave Berkley has the answer to that: "When a turkey comes all the way to an orange-headed decoy he is 20 yards from a hunter with a loaded shotgun. The bird should not live to remember anything at all."

5

HOW TO TALK TURKEY

"There's one call that you hear turkeys making all the time that very few hunters ever imitate," Jim Clay declared one morning as we drove out into the Virginia turkey woods.

"What's that?" I asked, surprised to hear such a claim.

"The cluck," Jim answered. "Turkey hens cluck more than they ever yelp or cackle. They walk around in the woods clucking. They cluck when they're on a roost, they cluck when they're feeding, and they cluck to communicate with other turkeys. Yet most turkey hunters put all their effort into yelping, cutting, and cackling and never cluck at all."

"You really think that's true?" I questioned, mentally reviewing my own turkey-calling repertoire and finding it admittedly deficient in the cluck department.

"I know it is," Jim said. "When I make that statement at turkey-calling seminars the hunters all look at each other and their jaws drop. They don't cluck." Jim Clay won the World All-Around Turkey Calling Championship in 1989 and 1990; he's also president of Perfection Turkey Calls, Inc., the company that first produced the now very popular multireed diaphragm mouth calls. He hunts turkeys and meets with groups of turkey hunters all over the nation. He knows what turkeys and turkey hunters do in the woods.

That day I listened carefully to how Jim's calls varied from what I'd heard from less experienced hunters. I found that there was a distinct difference. Jim opened with the usual yelps and cackles, but when he got a gobbler to respond he switched to soft, contented clucks, and when the gobbler homed in on us Jim clucked him all the way in to a range of about 10 feet.

It wasn't the cluck's fault that the gobbler was 10 feet behind us instead of out in front and that we were pinned down and couldn't move. Jim's clucking had brought him in just fine.

I have spent a lot of time hunting with turkey-calling champions and turkey-call manufacturers, and what impresses me most about their techniques is not their grand mastery of turkey-calling instruments but their restraint. These are men who make their livings designing, manufacturing, and using the calls that best imitate the sounds turkeys make—and yet when they're in the turkey woods they don't regale the birds with the fancy routines that win turkey-calling championships and entertain hunters at turkey-calling seminars.

Instead, once they have located a gobbler and gotten him answering, they frequently either switch to imitating the soft, contented sounds hen turkeys make when they're feeding or even go entirely silent.

One day I was in Missouri with Marc Drury, a six-time world turkey-calling champion and founder of M.A.D. Calls, Inc. Marc had a gobbler thundering on a ridge about 200 yards away. I fully expected him to hammer that turkey with a gorgeous rendition of the calls that had won him championships, but he didn't.

Instead Marc purred and clucked a few times and then went absolutely silent. When the gobbler boomed at us Marc just smiled and didn't make a sound. He whispered, "That's an old gobbler. He'll stay right there and gobble back at us all day if we get into a conversation with him. But it's late in the morning, and he's probably lost his hens. If I go quiet he may come looking for us."

The next time we heard the gobbler he was closer. Marc winked and nodded at me. He made a couple of very simple clucks and purrs. Then this expert turkey caller poked his diaphragm call into his cheek, laid his friction call in the leaves, and didn't make another peep.

When that gobbler appeared he was 35 yards away. He wasn't strutting, he was sneaking, looking for the hen that, by her rude silence, had indicated she was not going to run to him.

"There's times when going silent is more effective than continued calling," Marc declared.

In Kansas I hunted with Marc Scroggins, a well-known young turkey-calling champion—he ranked eighth in the 1997 World Turkey Calling Championship—who spends three months a year calling gobblers in extra close and filming their behavior for his Cross Timbers Video company.

We were hunting out of John and Pauline Doty's Shadow Oaks outfitting ranch in the rolling tallgrass prairie country near Sedan, where the big pastures are cut by deep, timbered draws and populations of both Eastern and Rio Grande turkeys thrive.

The weather had turned warm after a long cold spell. The turkeys were breaking up from their wintering flocks and spreading out all over the countryside.

Before dawn that first morning we set up near where we had heard a single gobbler sound off on his roost the previous evening.

As the morning light grew and the owls stopped hooting, gobblers began announcing themselves all around us. There were 15 different gobblers within earshot.

Marc opened with some soft yelping to establish that there was a hen here. Once it sounded like the closest gobblers had flown down he stepped up his calling, belting out several aggressive runs of cutts and insistent yelps. As soon as he'd gotten a gobbler to answer every call he backed off on the excitement level of his calling and made his yelps sound softer and more plaintive. As long as the gobbler kept answering and coming closer, Marc kept reducing the frequency, volume, and excitement level of his calling, making the gobbler come searching for the hen.

I killed that turkey at less than 20 yards when he hopped up on a rock to look for the maker of the sounds.

"You've gotta take a turkey's temperature," Marc explained. "If a gobbler is really hot and excited you can hammer right back at him, and he'll keep coming. But as he gets closer you want to stop calling aggressively and get subtle. Don't let him think you're a hen that is so hot she's going to run right to him. Make him hunt for the hen."

The professional turkey guides, call manufacturers, and videographers I've hunted with say that most turkey hunters call either too much or too little. A hunter who's not confident in his ability to talk turkey does not call enough and does not put enough emotion into his calling; once a hunter does gain confidence he often calls too much.

"You don't have to do anything fancy to call turkeys successfully," says Jim Clay. "Turkeys make all sorts of different sounds and most people learn to make sounds that are realistic enough right away. Calling in the right cadence is more important than the exact sound you make."

Cadence, the particular rhythmic sequence turkeys use to communicate vocally, has been made much easier to learn thanks to

Turkeys make all sorts of sounds. Calling in the right cadence is more important than the exact sound you make. Listen to recordings of actual turkey talk to learn the correct rhythm.

audiocassette recordings that are offered for sale by companies like Perfection Calls (Box 164, Stephenson, VA 22656, 540-667-4608) and M.A.D. Calls (1595 County Road 256, Columbia, MO 65202, 314-474-4516). These are excellent recordings of real wild turkeys communicating in the woods under genuinely wild conditions. Any turkey hunter will benefit by practicing the cadences and the sounds heard on them.

"A good caller knows how to put emotion in his calls," says Marc Scroggins. "A tree yelp should sound sleepy. A lost-hen yelp should sound lonesome. Clucks and purrs are contented, but cutts and cackles should be strident and sort of angry." The best way to learn to make those calls is to practice while listening to a tape recording of real turkey sounds.

"Plenty of hunters kill turkeys without knowing how to do anything but make yelping sounds with a box call," Jim Clay admits. "If a man just learns to make one call, but makes it sound good and uses the right cadence, he won't win calling championships, but he can be a very effective turkey caller in the woods."

The typical pattern of calls for an early-morning hunt opens with a short series of sleepy-sounding tree yelps to let a roosted gobbler know where you are. If the gobbler answers give him a louder series of yelps and then shut up. If you continue to yelp to a gobbler still in his tree he'll just keep gobbling, demanding that you go to him. If you shut up he may fly down and head your way. You don't want to call much while the gobbler is still on his limb.

Once you either have heard him fly down or can tell from the muffled sound of his call that he has dropped out of his tree and is on the ground, it's time to make your play. Make a few pleading yelps, then follow up with a short burst of cackling (use the fly-down cackle), beating your hat or your gloved hand against your leg as you make the call to simulate the sounds of beating wings.

Now that he is on the ground, the next time the gobbler answers give him back a strong series of impassioned yelps, beginning and ending with the abrupt, sharp *tutt* sounds that turkey callers call cutts. Then lay down your call and get your gun ready. Have a diaphragm call in your mouth to purr and cluck with if the gobbler hangs up on his way to you. Make scratching sounds with your hand in the leaves to encourage him. If he's coming your way be quiet and make him look for you.

If he fails to come all the way or fades off, step up the pitch and excitement level of your calling and keep pleading to him with yelps, cackles, and cutts until he turns your way again. As he begins to approach slack off the calling and make him hunt for you.

If the gobbler is with other hens he probably will not leave them and come to you. But another gobbler traveling with him, or one you may not know is around, may come in, so don't be too quick to get discouraged or change position.

Sometimes a gobbler in the company of hens can be brought into shooting range by making his dominant hen so angry that she comes over to drive you away and inadvertently drags the gobbler along with her.

Enraging the dominant hen to this degree requires a lot of aggressive cackling, yelping, and cutting. Give her back whatever she is saying to you—the same calls, same cadence, same number of repetitions.

Sometimes it works.

The easiest call to use is the box call. Anyone can get good sounds from a well-made box call if it is kept chalked and dry and is held by the base, with the fingers kept away from the sides of the box. Lots of hunters never use anything else.

Nevertheless, professional turkey callers agree that the more ways you have to vary your sounds, the better your chances of success.

After you've mastered the use of a box call, a push-button call is probably the next easiest to use. It makes soft purrs, and angry purrs depending on how hard you push the button, and is a great addition to a box call. Two push-button calls can be used together to mimic the angry purring sounds of two turkeys fighting; this is often a lethal technique for firing up a reluctant dominant gobbler or a dominant hen with a male escort.

A new type of friction call has become so popular in the past two years that it has almost entirely replaced the old wood and slate calls. The new product features a round plastic or metal resonating pot covered with a surface of glass, crystal, slate, or metal that produces very loud yelps, cutts, cackles, purrs, and clucks when scratched with a wood, glass, or carbon striker.

These new friction calls require a bit of practice before you know exactly how much pressure to apply and what to do with which striker, but once you do they are capable of making sounds that excite turkeys at long range or close up. The metal-faced calls are also waterproof when paired with a carbon striker.

"Sometimes gobblers will answer friction calls when they won't answer anything else," the expert callers with whom I've hunted agree.

The mouth diaphragm call is undoubtedly the most difficult turkey call to operate—but also the most convenient, once its capabilities have been mastered.

The secret is to position the diaphragm's short reed down halfway between your soft palate and your front teeth, seal the peripheral tape to the roof of your mouth so that no air leaks around it, and grunt air up from your chest while your jaw drops slightly as you say the words "rowf-rowf-rowf" or "kee-yok, kee-yok, kee-yok" to make a good yelp; "tak-tak-tak" for a cackle; or "puk-puk-puk" for a cutt. To make a convincing purring turkey sound, intone a high-pitched "prrrt-prrrt-prrrt" while you vibrate the tip of your tongue against the latex reeds.

Only after a lot of practice will you know what sound is going to come out of your mouth when you use a diaphragm call, but practice makes perfect. Single-reed calls and plain double-reed calls are easiest for beginners to get the hang of. As your proficiency increases you will be able to get an even wider variety of sounds from stacked multireed calls with specially shaped cuts in the reeds. Every individual has a unique shape to his mouth, so diaphragm calls sound different, depending on who is using them. You have to experiment to find which ones work best for you.

Mouth calls are perfect for times when a turkey is close enough to see the movement of your hands operating a call. Master mouth callers can say just about everything a turkey can say without ever having to move their hands.

"I'm a pretty good mouth caller but when I go turkey hunting I carry every type of call I own," says Jim Clay. "You never know exactly what a gobbler wants to hear and it helps to be able to make the widest possible range of sounds."

Real turkey noises are clear and mellow with a raspy edge to the sound and a definite break in the tone.

Once you've mastered the art of turkey calling it is natural to begin calling too much. The way to get over this tendency is to listen to what you hear in the woods. Most of the time turkeys are silent. When they speak they do so intermittently, with long periods of silence between calls.

Your goal should be to call loudly enough and frequently enough to get answers, but not so much that you give a gobbler the impression you're excited enough to run to him. If you call too much, the gobbler will stand his ground and gobble, wanting you to go to him. You want to create the impression that you're ready and willing, but not likely to chase after his attentions.

"Don't call too much," warns Jim Clay. "Just tell the gobbler where you are and keep him interested, but make him hunt to find you. That's easiest to accomplish if you can get ahead of him and call from the direction he's heading in anyway."

Most turkey hunters call either too much or too little. You should call enough to get a gobbler's attention and keep him interested, but don't get into a conversation with him. Go silent when he gets close, and make him hunt for you.

Hunters often worry that turkeys become call-shy after they have been duped a few times and have either been shot at or come in to a call and seen the hunter. The turkey-calling pros don't give much importance to call-shyness, though.

"Turkeys have to breed," Jim Clay points out. "To find each other they rely on calls. If your calling is realistic and you call sparingly, just like the way turkeys call to one another, you can overcome a turkey's natural wariness. You just have to sound real and give him time to come in slowly.

"And remember," Jim cautions, "you're not supposed to get a turkey every time you go. Go out there to learn about turkeys and be patient. You'll kill one soon enough."

6

MAKING YOUR OWN TURKEY CALLS

Making your own turkey calls is a sure way to extend the pleasure of the hunt into the off-season months. Mike Morton (5249 Calion Highway, El Dorado, AR 71730, 501-862-5972), who makes all of his calls himself, says that making his own turkey calls is at least half the fun of turkey hunting.

Mike is a retired school principal who now makes handcrafted, hand-painted, custom duck, goose, and turkey calls that combine such unique tonal quality and artistic beauty that they have become collector's items among knowledgeable hunters. Mike says that anyone with a sincere interest and normal woodworking skills can make calls that turkeys like to hear—and have fun doing it.

"When you're making a call you just know it's going to be a special one," he says. "Every call you make puts you in the turkey woods

Mike Morton says that making your own turkey calls is at least half the fun of turkey hunting.

while you're working on it. In your mind's eye you can see the turkey coming in while you shape the wood. You can hear him gobble and drum each time you make some trial sounds with the call you're working on. I kill a lot of turkeys in my head when I'm making turkey calls. The turkeys never turn you down on these imaginary hunts."

Mike has been hunting with calls he made himself for most of his hunting life. He has a raspy cedar box call he made years ago that has notches up and down the edges of its base, marking turkeys that have succumbed to it. He carries a flute-toned wing-bone call made from the bones of a hen turkey he killed one autumn, but the calls he uses most are slate-faced friction calls that he makes from easily obtainable materials.

WHERE TO GET MATERIALS AND HOW TO CONSTRUCT

To make a turkey call you need very dry wood. Mike says the cheapest source of fine-grained, very dry wood is pieces of old furni-

To make a turkey call you need a source of very dry, fine-grained wood. Excellent working material can be obtained from pieces of old broken furniture.

ture that are no longer useful. Furniture is generally made from the very best tight-grained wood, and tight grain is what gives a call its tone. The legs and tops of older tables are gems for turkey-call making; they're made of maple, walnut, cherry, mahogany, poplar, basswood—old, fully cured, tight-grained wood that you could not find for sale or, if you did, would cost you dearly, and is just waiting to be picked up at the dump or in the attic.

Use a band saw to saw the wood lengthwise (with the grain) into broad strips ¼ and ⅛ inch thick, and store them in a dry place for call making. Once you work up a good supply of pieces you will find yourself wondering what kind of tone you'll get from various combinations of your wood supply; the next thing you know you'll be in the shop putting together a call that you just know is going to be a winner.

SLATE-FACED FRICTION CALLS

For slate-faced friction calls Mike Morton uses natural slate that he gathers along the roadside where highway construction cuts through slate veins. He picks up thin pieces that have a tight grain, then files and sands them to an even ⅛-inch thickness. If he can't find natural slate he buys pieces of the ⅛-inch-thick slate tiles avail-

Slate Call

1. Measure and cut. To make a 2" by 3" box from $\frac{1}{8}$" stock, be sure to subtract $\frac{1}{4}$" from the length of both end pieces.

2. Glue corners with epoxy, and clamp with rubberbands or a small C-clamp until glue sets.

$\frac{5}{8}$" hole

$\frac{1}{4}$" hole

3. Cut a piece of $\frac{1}{8}$" slate to 2" by 3". Drill four $\frac{5}{16}$" holes as shown. Be sure to back up the slate with scrap wood when drilling.

4. For the striker, drill a $\frac{5}{8}$" hole $\frac{3}{4}$" deep into the end of a $1\frac{1}{4}$" diameter by $2\frac{1}{2}$" hardwood dowel. Drill a $\frac{1}{4}$" hole through the length of the dowel from the center of the $\frac{5}{8}$" hole. Drive an 8" piece of hardwood dowel through the center hole.

Illustration by Clarke Barre

able at stores that sell tiles for floors and countertops. Sand them smooth with fine-grained sandpaper.

To assemble a slate-faced friction call Mike constructs a simple 2-inch by 3-inch wooden frame, using 1-inch-wide, ⅛-inch-thick strips of tight-grained wood from his selected wood supply. He glues the four corners with epoxy glue and holds them together with clamps or rubber bands while the glue dries.

When the box is completed Mike uses a hacksaw to cut a 2-inch by 3-inch piece of ⅛-inch-thick slate and glues this to the top of the box, holding it in place with clamps or rubber bands until dry (about an hour).

Now he sands the corners and edges to make the call feel nice in the hand.

To make the striker handle Mike saws off a 2½-inch piece of 1¼-inch-diameter hardwood dowel of the type sold in hardware stores and lumberyards for use as closet rods. Next he drills a ⅝-inch-diameter hole ¾ inch into the center of one end of the piece of dowel to create a resonance chamber. Then he drills a ¼-inch-diameter hole from the center of the hole he just drilled, through the center of the length of the piece of dowel.

To make the striker peg he cuts an 8-inch-long piece of ¼-inch-diameter hardwood dowel and drives it through the ¼-inch hole he drilled in the striker handle until it protrudes about 1½ inches from one end of the handle, leaving about 4 inches protruding from the other end. Later the tone of the call can be adjusted by moving the striker handle farther up or down on the peg.

To tune the call Mike practices to see what sounds he can get from it and tries to find a "sweet spot," where there is a tonal break that gives the call a special yelping quality. Sometimes he experiments by drilling two to four holes of various diameters through the slate surface to change the tonal range.

If he wants to beef the call up he glues on a very thin 2-inch by 3-inch wooden back. Then he plays with it to see what it will do.

"Every call is different in tone and has a different point where the tone breaks," Mike says. "The more you practice with it, the better you will be able to run it. I haven't made a call yet that you couldn't get some good turkey sounds out of. Every time you make one it gives you ideas for something a little different. I wind up giving a lot of calls away to hunting friends while I keep searching for the call of all calls."

BOX CALLS

To make box calls Mike goes back to his hoard of call-making wood. He chooses ¼-inch-thick stock to make the bottom and the top paddle, and ⅛-inch-thick stock for the sides.

"The best way to make a box call is to copy one," Mike says. "After you've copied one call and experienced putting the pieces together you know how it's done. Then you can experiment with different lengths and widths to suit your fancy.

"There's not much to the construction," Mike adds. "You just need to recess the sides into ⅛-inch channels you cut in the bottom, and use blocks of various dimensions at both ends to hold the sides and bottom together.

"You want to use tight-grained, thoroughly dry wood throughout, but you can use all sorts of combinations of woods to make box calls that sound wonderful. If you want to use cedar sides you can buy the kind of cedar paneling they sell at the lumberyard for paneling closets. Almost any wood you take from old furniture will make interesting sounds."

The tonal break in a box call comes from the curved top edge of its sides. Most box-call sides are curved at the top from end to end so that the sides are about ¼ inch higher in the center than they are at the ends.

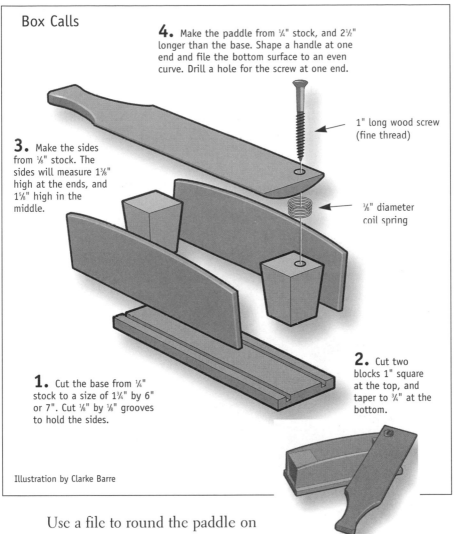

Box Calls

4. Make the paddle from ¼" stock, and 2½" longer than the base. Shape a handle at one end and file the bottom surface to an even curve. Drill a hole for the screw at one end.

1" long wood screw (fine thread)

3. Make the sides from ⅛" stock. The sides will measure 1⅜" high at the ends, and 1⅝" high in the middle.

⅜" diameter coil spring

1. Cut the base from ¼" stock to a size of 1¾" by 6" or 7". Cut ⅛" by ⅛" grooves to hold the sides.

2. Cut two blocks 1" square at the top, and taper to ¾" at the bottom.

Illustration by Clarke Barre

Use a file to round the paddle on the bottom side, and prepare to attach it to the block at one end of the box by drilling a small hole near the end of the paddle, centered between the edges.

To attach the paddle to the block, pass a fine-threaded, 1-inch-long screw through the hole you drilled near the end of the paddle and then through a ½-inch section of ⅜-inch-diameter coil spring, which you must insert between the paddle and the end block. Then continue to turn the screw into the end block. The spring is used to stabilize the tension on the paddle as it is scraped over the top edges of the box sides to make turkey sounds.

WING-BONE CALLS

Every turkey hunter should carry a wing-bone call, if only because it's a traditional call that is made from the best of all sources: the wild turkey itself.

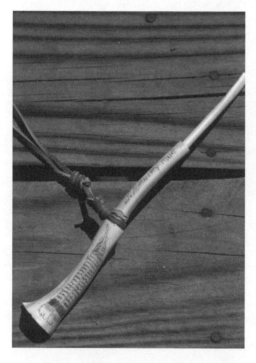

To make one remove the bones from the two heaviest joints of a turkey's wing. (Some hunters say that wing bones from hen turkeys killed during the autumn "either-sex" hunting season make the most realistic sounds.)

Scrape the flesh from the three bones, then boil them for half an hour. Once all remaining flesh from the outside of the bones is boiled off use a hacksaw to cut 4 inches from the thickest section of each of the three bones. Then saw off the closed joint faces in order to create an open-ended flared end at the thickest end of each bone.

A wing-bone call like this is made from the three large bones in a turkey's wing. They are boiled clean then fitted together and cemented with epoxy. Kissing sounds made through the small end come out as turkey yelps and clucks.

Now use a stiff wire with a cloth swab attached to clean out all marrow from inside the bone sections.

Once the bone sections are as clean as you can get them, sand each piece with fine-grit emery cloth until very smooth—or buff them on an electric wheel. Now slide the three sections together telescope-fashion until they lock tight. There is no need for the sections to overlap by more than ⅛ inch, so take the call apart and trim off any excess length in the overlap section.

Once you have a fit that does not includes overlaps of more than ⅛ inch, you are ready to glue the sections together using epoxy glue or fiberglass resin. Seal the joints with glue on both the inside and the outside. When the glue dries sand off any excess that may have accumulated on the outside of the joints.

To dress up a wing-bone call you might use a needle or etching point to scratch decorative designs on its outside. Then apply india ink to the scratch marks, wipe away all excess ink, and give the call a coat of varnish or epoxy resin to seal its surface.

If the final result is too shiny you can dull it with a quick wipe with steel wool.

MOUTH DIAPHRAGM CALLS

Thanks to the M.A.D Calls company you can now make your own mouth diaphragm calls, too. Its Call Maker is a complete kit that enables turkey hunters to make their own custom mouth diaphragm calls at a fraction of the normal cost. The kit includes a heavy duty aluminum mounting jig and enough materials to make 10 four-reed mouth calls. It comes with an instructional video-cassette that shows exactly how to put calls together and how to vary them for different effects.

Materials refills are available. Easy to use and conveniently portable, the Call Maker sells for $49.95 (see page 45 for address).

"Every turkey hunter should make his own calls," says Mike Morton. "It's really a thrill to call in a turkey with a call you made yourself."

7

HUNTING THE HUSHED-MOUTH TURKEY

" I've never seen more turkey sign—or heard less gobbling." That's the lament heard each spring from hunters in every state where wild turkey populations are peaking.

As wild turkeys reach new population highs across North America hunters almost everywhere are claiming that turkeys are gobbling less than they used to. Whether you're hunting the Osceola subspecies in Florida, the Rio Grande in Texas, the Merriam in the Black Hills, or the Eastern turkey in, say, Georgia, you will hear the same disheartening complaint. "Turkeys just don't gobble like they used to."

Most hunters have a theory on why the birds are gobbling less, and several of the theories carry serious scientific weight. Here are three worth considering:

1. Turkeys that gobble frequently draw more attention to themselves and are the first to be pursued by both hunters and predators. As the most talkative birds are killed off, those that are genetically inclined to be less vocal are left to do more of the breeding. Hence we are selectively breeding less vocal turkeys.

2. Wherever hunting pressure is heavy, birds become spooked and are less likely to advertise their presence by gobbling. As the number of turkey hunters increases, turkeys encounter hunters in the woods more often and become accordingly more wary and less vocal.

3. When turkey populations reach the carrying capacity of a range there is a natural reduction in breeding activity. Since there is no longer any need to expand the population nature dictates that fewer turkeys actually breed; there is a noticeable drop in the numbers of both male and female turkeys that mate or show interest in seeking each other during the breeding season — hence lots of turkeys, but less gobbling.

Of course it's also true that today's turkey hunters, many of whom are relatively new to the sport, may have unrealistic expectations regarding how much gobbling activity they should hear. When gobblers are actively breeding and traveling with hens that stay with them all day, they don't have to gobble to attract company. There are always hushed-mouth periods when most gobblers don't talk.

"People tend to remember stories in which the hunter plies his turkey-calling skills against an old gobbler that renders judgment of the caller's abilities by gobbling," notes former Georgia wildlife director Jack Crockford. "They forget about the days when nobody heard anything."

Nevertheless, Jack Crockford agreed that he had never seen more turkey sign than in the spring of 1997, nor heard less gobbling in his favorite hunting grounds. "They're just not saying anything,"

When gobblers are with hens, they sometimes go silent and may not respond to calling. Even at the height of the breeding season there are "hushed-mouth" periods when most gobblers won't talk.

Jack said after three days of hard hunting in the steep mountains of the Chattahoochee National Forest. "It's the worst I've ever seen."

Down in Sumter County, Florida, former sheriff Jamie Adams, who now wears the hat of that state's National Wild Turkey Federation Osceola Chapter chairman, says, "We've had to change the way we hunt 'em."

Osceola turkeys have always been notable for their extra wariness and have a reputation for a tendency to gobble less than other subspecies, but Jamie Adams says it's gotten worse. "If you're lucky they'll gobble from their tree at daybreak, but when they hit the ground they go silent. It's like hunting ghosts."

So what's a hunter to do? Nobody ever said that turkey hunting was easy, even when the birds let you know where they were. Hunting ghosts is even harder.

"You gotta know your bird," says Sheriff Adams. "Know where he wants to be and get there ahead of him. If you see a bird strutting in a certain place mark it down as a known strutting place and plan to set up on him there another day. Be patient. Call from time to time to let him know you're there and be still. 'Cause when he comes in he may not say a word, he'll just suddenly be there, and you best be ready."

Knowing where turkeys want to be is the most important factor in successfully hunting hushed-mouth turkeys.

Danny Pierce has made a business out of knowing where the local Rio Grande turkeys want to be. Danny operates Rush Creek

Knowing where turkeys want to be is the most important factor in successfully hunting hushed-mouth turkeys. Go to a place you know a gobbler wants to be, call softly from time to time, and wait for him.

Guide Service (Box 41, Reydon, OK 73660, 405-655-4690) and has more than 20,000 acres of prime Rio habitat under lease on both sides of the Texas-Oklahoma border.

"When turkeys are quiet, you can either move around calling here and there to see if you can luck out and strike one that will respond to a call, or you can go to a place you know a gobbler wants to be and wait for him," Danny advises. "Put out decoys, call occasionally to let him know you're there, and wait for the gobbler to move into range of your calling. When he hears you in his chosen place chances are very good that he'll come in."

How do you know where a turkey wants to be?

"Observation," says Danny. "Scratch marks and droppings tell you where turkeys have been feeding recently. Lots of droppings under certain trees identify roosting trees. Feathers on the ground indicate where breeding or fighting has occurred and these places should be remembered as probable strut zones. Wherever you see turkeys at certain hours remember the time and place because they're likely to be there again. If you see groups of hens they are being tended by a gobbler that is nearby and may be callable if you can get close to him, even if he does not respond to calls coming from a distance."

Wherever you see turkeys at certain hours, remember the time and place because they're likely to be there at the same hour another day.

Four turkey hunters I met one evening in a Nebraska rodeo town told me they had about given up on the local Merriam turkeys. "We're not hearing anything," they said. "Been here all week, and we haven't had one turkey answer a call."

"The gobblers are traveling with hens right now," explained Nebraska's Ponderosa Wildlife Management Area superintendent Lon Lemmon. "They don't have to gobble because the hens are staying with them all day and roosting with them at night."

One morning I climbed high into the peaks of Nebraska's Pine Ridge, which is the southern terminus of South Dakota's Black Hills, and searched for turkeys. There was sign everywhere, but even though I was on hand before daylight I heard no turkey sounds, and by 9 A.M. no turkeys had come to my calls. So I went looking. I stayed in the cover of timber and occasionally peeked out into the wide-open alpine parks and highland pastures to which my route led me.

Eventually I did spot a flock—six hens, a jake, and two big longbeards—in a food plot planted way out in a mountain pasture. The hens were feeding, and the gobblers were standing around in full strut, displaying their wares.

I watched the flock for nearly an hour before they began to move slowly to the north. By ducking into cover and moving fast I was able to move around to the north end of the pasture and set out decoys in a low saddle I felt sure they would use to exit the open country.

Then, hidden by a bulge in the terrain, I settled back against a ponderosa trunk and began to call. No answers. Eventually the turkeys moved to where I could see them, but what I saw was not pleasing. The whole flock—hens, jake, and longbeards—would look my way when I called, and they could see the decoys, but they were veering away from rather than being attracted toward me.

They were not acting frightened, but it was clear that they were not going to come closer, either.

"In a situation like that the hens are in charge," Lon Lemmon explained later. "They have a close-knit little breeding group and they don't necessarily want to join any strange hens. Those hens veered off rather than coming to your calls and decoys because they probably wanted to keep their gobblers to themselves. The gobblers just follow along and go where the hens go in that situation."

8

THE
BUFFER
ZONE

Steve Stoltz of St. Louis, Missouri, believes that wild turkeys have two buffer zones that determine when they will respond to calling. Steve films hunting episodes for the Drury Outdoor Company and is the 1993 World Turkey Calling Champion. This means he can please the ears of the most demanding human judges. But Steve also wins when it comes to pleasing the most difficult judge of all—the long-spurred, long-bearded, mature wild turkey. He is a master turkey caller.

Steve is convinced that turkeys maintain two zones of private space around them. There is a fairly wide zone in which a turkey will salute you when you call from within its borders; there is also a much smaller critical primary zone that extends roughly 60 to 70 yards from the turkey. He will investigate any calls that come from within the latter circle.

"If you can call from within 60 yards of the turkey he will come looking for you," Steve declares. "If you call from within the much wider secondary zone he will probably answer your calls and may or may not come looking for you.

"Even when gobblers are with hens they will usually break away and investigate hen sounds that come from within 60 yards," Steve says.

But it's getting to within 60 yards of a turkey without spooking him that is the trick.

Steve gets in close by moving through the turkey woods slowly, stopping to call every 30 to 50 yards. At his stops he makes a short series of aggressive yelps and ends with sharp cutts. Then he follows with another short series of louder cutts.

"Hens cutt when they are ready to breed," Steve explains. "A

Steve Stoltz believes that every gobbler has a primary buffer zone. If you can get within that zone the gobbler will answer and may come to your calls. Steve moves through the woods slowly, cutting every 30 to 50 yards, until he crosses the line into a gobbler's zone and gets an answer.

gobbler that has hens with him will usually leave his hens to look for an unseen hen that is cutting from within his primary zone and sometimes will even go looking for a hen he hears cutting within his secondary zone."

By stopping to make the cutting calls every 30 to 50 yards as he moves through the woods, Steve expects eventually to cross the line into the zone in which a turkey will respond.

"This is a good way to locate turkeys when they have gone silent," he says. "If you don't know where the gobbler is your best bet is to move around slowly and quietly in places you know he uses, stopping to call every 30 to 50 yards. When you cross into his secondary zone you'll know it—he'll answer.

"The turkey may only answer the call one time," Steve continues. "That is just a 'courtesy answer.' If he answers your call twice he may be willing to come to you, so pick a good spot to sit, put out your decoys, and start working him. You may be able to get him to come all the way to you. If he answers but doesn't come, you'll have to move closer."

I saw Steve work his system on a memorable hunt in northern Missouri in the spring of 1997. We had roosted the bird the night before and knew that he was in a small patch of timber surrounded by open fields in hilly terrain. The next morning we crept in under the cover of darkness and set up within 60 to 70 yards of his tree at the edge of an open hay field. We set the decoys, a hen and a little jake, 20 yards out in the field and then crawled into a tiny patch of weeds along the fence line.

We were counting on the bird either pitching down directly into the field or dropping out of his tree and walking uphill toward us, with the decoys in view pulling him past us.

About 15 minutes before fly-down time Steve gave out a short, soft series of tree yelps. A couple of minutes later he repeated the series, but added three sharp cutts at the end, signaling that the hen the gobbler was hearing was eager to breed. Then Steve went silent. The gobbler, however, went wild, double-gobbling and triple-gobbling his demands that the hen move to him.

As daylight grew stronger we could hear hens rustling in the trees below us. Eventually one flew out and set her wings; we could see her glide all the way to an open field at the bottom of the hill, landing several hundred yards from us. Next several more hens were heard flying out of their trees. They, too, pitched out away from us and glided to the distant field.

Now came the telling moment. Would the gobbler follow them?

Steve belted out three sharp cutts. *Tac-tac—tac!*

That did it. We heard the heavy wings of the gobbler as he pitched out in our direction.

"He's coming," Steve whispered. "He didn't follow the hens. He wants the hen he hears over here."

What followed was classic turkey hunting. I generally prefer to do my own calling, but when I am in the presence of experts I know enough to keep my calls in my pocket, shut up, listen, and learn.

Although Steve had been mostly silent when the gobbler was in his tree, calling only enough to let the gobbler know where he was and planting the suggestion that he was a breedable hen, once the gobbler was on the ground Steve stepped up the pace.

He hit hard with an aggressive series of yelps and cutts and, when the gobbler boomed back his demand that the hen go to him, Steve went silent. When the gobbler called again a minute later, saying, "I'm here. Come to me," Steve remained silent, making the gobbler wonder where the hen had gone.

They played this game for nearly half an hour. Steve would excite the gobbler with aggressive cutting then go silent, frustrating the bird with his apparent disappearance or loss of interest. Then, before the gobbler's ardor flagged, he would give out another burst of passionate cutting.

But this was an old bird. He was cautious. It became clear that he would stand his ground; he was not going to come up the hill and into our view. He was insisting that the hen go to him and indicating that he was not going to let his ardor make him incautious.

"We've got to relocate," Steve whispered. "He's not going to come to this place."

So we pulled back on our bellies, picked up the decoys, and used terrain to hide us as we circled around to the left and out of sight. Then we crossed the fence into the timber and dropped downhill, using a bulge in the terrain to keep us from being seen.

Once we were down on the gobbler's elevation level we began creeping toward him. We knew exactly where the bird was located, and the terrain and brushy cover allowed us to get in very close.

"We're well inside his primary zone now," Steve whispered to me. "He's just around the edge of this little hill. We're too close to go any farther so we can't get a decoy out in front of us. Sit in front of me with your gun up and don't move a hair."

I got into position as quietly as I could and nodded when I was ready.

Steve yelped, then cutt. The gobbler exploded with a double gobble.

When Steve purred back and emitted a soft cluck, there was no response. Steve clucked again. Still silence.

"He's coming," Steve whispered. "When they stop responding and they're this close, they're coming in."

I saw the bird a moment later. Rather, I should say I saw the bird's head. A spot of white had appeared suddenly where no white spot had been before. For seconds it didn't move. But finally it did move, and when it did I saw the eye, the gray snood dangling beside the beak. Then, briefly, I saw black feathers move. Steve made no sound. This turkey was committed. We were inside his primary zone, and he was looking for us.

The bird was not displaying. He withheld his colors, coming toward us one tiny step at a time with his head camouflaged in gray and his feathers slick. He was sneaking in, suspicious that something was wrong. He was ready to flee, but he was unable to resist searching for the hen he had heard within his primary zone.

Never did a bird move more slowly. He would take a step, then stop and survey his domain from this new position, moving only his head as he looked things over from various eye levels. Then one more tiny step.

I never saw the whole bird. He used the cover of tree trunks and brush to keep himself hidden as he closed in on our location. But at one point he stopped where I could see his chest, and the rope of a beard that sprouted from it gave me the same sense of gratification I have felt watching the rack of a trophy buck come toward me through the woods.

The bird was less than 30 yards away when he stepped behind the trunk of a large oak, which completely hid him.

I used that moment when he was hidden to adjust my gun position; now I held the bead on the left side of the tree, level with his head. When his head and neck appeared and I saw that big beard coming into view, I put the bead on his wattles and squeezed off the shot.

"That bird was not going to leave us unless he saw us move," Steve explained later. "Once we got within his primary zone he was committed to finding the hen. But he was going to do it his way. Slowly. Cautiously. If we could have had a decoy out to give him an explanation of where the sounds were coming from he would have strutted and come right in. But as long as he couldn't see the hen he was wary.

"I don't know why he wouldn't come to our original location," Steve added. "But when a bird refuses to come to one place, you've got to move to a new position and see if he will come there."

When he is moving through the woods trying to locate a turkey that has gone silent Steve uses an extra-high-frequency, M.A.D. Super Aluminator aluminum-faced friction call (see chapter 9) until he gets a response.

"I don't think the extra-high-frequency calls are better than a lot of other calls for bringing turkeys in, but they *are* the best things I've ever used for getting gobblers to answer. Once you get an answer you know where the turkey is and you can then work on him with whatever calls you like."

The first time a gobbler answers a call he stops and listens but usually does not start moving toward the call until he has answered several times.

"When you get an answer you should move toward the bird and get closer before you call again. You don't want the bird to start moving toward you before you're ready," Steve cautions. "The first answer tells you where a bird is. Next you should move about halfway to him. Then call again. If he answers get ready. He may come all the way. If he hangs up and stops moving toward you and refuses to budge but keeps on answering, you'll have to move in even closer. Use the terrain and cover to keep hidden, and move as close to him as you can. Sometimes you can move in a creek bed or stay behind a rise of ground and get very close. If you can get within 60 yards of a bird that keeps answering he's going to come to you.

"Lots of hunters make the mistake of thinking that when birds stop gobbling the hunt is over," Steve says. "Actually that's when the real hunt begins. When the birds are quiet you have to hunt for them. Once you know where a bird is you can work on him."

ROOSTING HABITS

You can get a good idea of whether or not a gobbler has hens with him by where he roosts, Steve Stoltz explains. Gobblers with hens usually roost low on the side of a hill and low in the tree they select. Gobblers without the company of hens roost high on ridges and high in their tree.

It makes sense. The bird that already has hens does not need to be in a position from which he can attract them the next morning. But gobblers without hens must roost in high locations from which they can be heard for a greater distance in order to attract hens come dawn.

"When you have a choice go for the bird that roosts high," Steve suggests. "He is the one that will be looking for company in the morning and will be most vulnerable to seductive calling."

9

SECRET SOUNDS THAT TURKEYS HEAR

Human ears can hear only about half the range of sounds that wild turkeys make when they communicate with one another. This means that turkey hunters may be hearing only half of what turkeys say, according to a study conducted in 1995 and 1996 by Marc Drury at the University of Missouri's speech and hearing department.

For years turkey hunters have been increasingly aware that high-pitched turkey calls seem to get more gobbling response than lower-toned, mellow calls. But nobody knew why.

Marc Drury decided to find out. He made dozens of tape recordings of wild turkeys communicating with one another and had them computer analyzed on a spectrogram machine, which measures frequency levels in hertz units.

Marc Drury and his associates at M.A.D. Calls spent many hours in the turkey woods testing which calls got the most answers from wild gobblers. Their discoveries launched the current rush to offer high-pitched calls that peak at very high frequencies.

He found that typical turkey sounds have a low–high range of 350 to a little over 15,000 hertz. In comparison, typical human speech patterns range from 2,000 to 4,000 hertz; the upper limit of human hearing is about 8,000 hertz. Telephones deliver speech sounds at a frequency level of 3,000 hertz.

"It is an accepted theory that species do not make sounds they cannot hear," Marc notes. "So we can assume that we are probably missing about half of the sounds turkeys make."

Marc Drury's company, M.A.D. Calls, has become a nationally recognized leader in the turkey-call industry in just three years. In 1994 he introduced the first "silent" turkey locator call. Similar to a silent dog whistle, the call produces very high-frequency sounds that surpass human hearing but have been proved to make turkeys gobble at long distances. It's particularly useful in the evening for locating roosting gobblers.

"The success of that very high-frequency call told me we were on to something, so I decided to find out what the range of turkey hearing really is," Marc says.

He also made spectrogram studies of the range of sounds produced by the most popular turkey calls on the market. He found that the most effective calls are those with the highest frequency range.

Consequently M.A.D. Calls introduced the Super Aluminator and the Super Crystal, two friction-type calls with acoustic-grade resonance chambers covered with faces of abraded aluminum or fine crystal that, when scraped with one of several custom-designed strikers, produce a full range of turkey sounds that peak at the very high frequency of more than 15,000 hertz.

Turkeys can communicate at frequencies that humans cannot hear. Calls like this M.A.D. Super Aluminator, which is designed to reach levels of 12,000 to 15,000 hertz, often make turkeys gobble even when they refuse to respond to lower-pitched calls.

Tested widely in the field during the 1996 spring gobbler season, the high-pitched sounds proved to draw far more gobbling responses than calls with lower-frequency ranges. They often brought responses from gobblers that remained silent when lower-frequency calls were used.

Calls that produce sounds that peak beyond the reach of human hearing have a distinct difference. You can tell that there's a lot more happening than you can hear. When I listen, beyond the lower-frequency sounds that I can hear I feel a sort of clicking pressure on my eardrum.

There is no question that turkeys hear and respond to the high-frequency sounds with a high degree of excitement from extra-long distances.

When I hunted with Marc Drury in May 1996 he and his team of testers were all carrying survey sheets on clipboards. Each time they worked a turkey they made test cutts, cackles, and yelps with three prototype turkey calls that produced peak frequencies of 5,000, 10,000, and 15,000 hertz, respectively. Time after time the highest-pitched call brought gobbling responses when the lower-frequency calls failed.

What does this information mean for turkey hunters?

"You're going to see turkey-call manufacturers scrambling to produce calls that will reach 15,000 hertz," Marc Drury predicts. "Every type of turkey call is going to be redesigned to increase its high-frequency range."

10

THE FLOATING CALLER

Even when you use decoys there are times when turkeys will come just so far and no closer. That happened one bright sunny afternoon on a ranch Danny Pierce had leased near Wheeler in the central panhandle of Texas. Rio Grande turkeys are abundant there near every timbered draw.

Marc Scroggins and his brother Steve had called up a big old longbeard whose hens had left him. They were attempting to pull him out of a large open pasture and within shotgun range of a fence line along the edge of heavy cover, where they sat fully camouflaged.

They had a hen decoy 20 yards out and a little to the left of their hide, and they counted on it to take the gobbler's eye off them when he came close.

To get stubborn gobblers to approach Marc Scroggins uses a two-man technique he calls the "floating caller." The caller drops back into the woods, leaving the shooter in place. As the sounds of the calls move away the gobbler may follow and walk into the silent shooter's range.

But Rios are a bird of open spaces. They feel safe when they can see what is around them; they're often spooked when required to leave the safety of the open to be pulled to the edge of heavy cover.

This old bird had a classic resistance to approaching heavy cover. He would hammer back at every call as he slowly made his way across the open pasture from some 300 yards away, but he stopped about 60 yards from the gun—too far for a sure killing shot.

Marc plied the bird with everything he had. In turkey talk he pleaded, begged, and promised passionate diversions, but the old bird stood his ground and strutted back and forth with a firm resolve that said: "If you want me, you come out here."

The Scroggins brothers quit calling for a while and let the big tom go back to feeding and wander off a short distance, then hit him again with calls that brought him trotting back toward them. Once more, though, the old bird stopped at 60 yards and would come no farther.

"He must have been ambushed before," Marc whispered to Steve. "It's time for a 'floating caller.'"

Again the brothers stopped calling and let the old bird cool down. Eventually the gobbler turned his back and began to feed away from them. When he passed over a bulge in the terrain that gave him momentary cover, Marc wormed his way out through the short grass on his belly and retrieved the decoy.

Now, with the decoy out of sight, he left Steve in position and crawled back into the cover of the timbered draw that lay behind him. About 40 yards into the cover behind Steve, Marc began plaintive calling.

At once the old gobbler stopped feeding and popped into full strut. Continuing to move slowly away from the bird and from his brother, who sat hidden at his original shooting position, Marc gave the old bird the impression that the passionate hen he kept hearing was moving away from him and refusing to come out into the field. The missing decoy confirmed that impression.

The old gobbler quickly returned to his original stopping place, gobbling all the way, and went into strut again. But by now Marc had drifted even farther back into the draw, calling seductively and "floating" to the left or right, as required to keep a straight line from himself through Steve's position to the ever-changing position of the bird. This way, if the bird broke and ran to him, he would run right over Steve.

When the old bird gobbled one more time Marc hit him with an aggressive series of cuts and loud yelps from 60 yards back in the timber.

That was too much for the old gobbler. He broke and started to trot toward the fence with the clear intention of going after the obstinate hen that had refused his ardor and was now retreating into the woods.

Steve stopped him at 20 yards.

"The floating caller works particularly well on birds that have been called into gun range before and managed to get away," Marc explained. "They get leery of situations that might be an ambush, and they'll just hang up where they feel safe and stand there demanding that the hen come to them. If you can create the impression that the hen is going away you can sometimes pull them close to a shooting position that they would not approach otherwise."

11

MASTERS
OF THE
CUT 'N' RUN

When turkeys are not gobbling, Marc Drury refuses to accept the rebuke and goes looking for one that will gobble. Marc has probably called up as many gobblers to the gun and the camera as any man in the field.

I was with him in 1996 hunting turkeys on public land in southern Missouri during one of those periods when the turkeys wouldn't talk.

"Remember," he told me, "we aren't hunting turkeys in general— we're hunting the single individual turkey that is alone and looking for female company.

"Most of the time," Marc continued, "turkeys are not gobbling. They may gobble on their roosts, but when they get on the ground with hens they often shut up for as long as the hens stay with them.

Even when most gobblers are "henned up" and unresponsive there is always one some-where that will come to a call. Marc Drury and Steve Stoltz don't wait for conditions to change—they go looking for the individual gobblers that are looking for company.

If that's what's happening on the day you want to hunt you can't wait for time to improve the situation—you have to go looking for a turkey that will play the game now."

With that we boarded Marc's Chevy pickup and began the fastest-moving turkey hunt I've ever experienced.

We whizzed down the gravel roads, braked to a stop wherever a hardwood ridge bulged out above a good-looking hollow, and dashed into the woods a little ways. Then Marc would whip out an aluminum-faced friction call and belt out a very aggressive series of cuts and yelps. He didn't mess around with soft introductions, he just got out of the truck and hammered.

"The law says we've got to quit hunting at 12:30," he reminded me. "Between now and then we've got to find a turkey that is alone and lonely. That's the one bird we want to find."

I suppose we covered 10 miles and made more than a dozen stops before we got an answer. But when that gobble came back at us Marc said, "That's him. Get your stuff."

We worked out to the end of the ridge, halfway to where the turkey had gobbled, before Marc called again. This time he was more polite. He called softly at first, then got louder when no answer came back from his opening gambit.

As soon as he reached a staccato-high frequency the turkey shot back a reply from the opposite ridge.

We crept halfway toward the gobbler, then crawled up against some windfallen debris. Marc went to work on him.

Marc is a great caller and perhaps it was his technique that brought that bird to us on a dead trot. But I think it was more than that. Marc had found a bird that was ready to work, and when you have a bird that wants to come to the call success is mostly a matter of not doing something wrong—such as moving, shooting too soon, or missing the bird when he runs in too close.

Marc Drury is a master of this cut 'n' run turkey-hunting technique. He never gets discouraged. When I missed one that came too close to the unfamiliar gun I was shooting Marc just said, "Let's go get another." And we did. Even though it was generally agreed in camp that evening that turkeys were not responding to calls, Marc had found two that morning that did respond and in fact came all the way to us.

"There's always a bird that's looking for company somewhere," he said. "It's just a matter of finding him."

Steve Stoltz is another master of the cut 'n' run.

In his job as a maker of hunting films Steve can't afford to wait for the great times when the hens leave the gobblers and turkeys gobble and respond to calls all day. He has to get out there and find birds that will respond when birds are generally unresponsive.

"Even on a good day turkeys only gobble about 20 percent of the time," Steve notes.

"If I can get a bird to answer I move in as close as I can before I start working him," he adds. "If the gobbler is with hens he probably will not leave them and move very far, but if you can work in close you may be able to tempt him to leave his hens and come investigate your calling."

LOCATOR CALLS

When you're planning to move close to a bird it's a good idea to use a stimulator that is not a turkey sound to locate him: He may move toward a turkey call and catch you in the act of sneaking in on him.

Steve Stoltz has had good luck locating gobblers by using a silent dog whistle that emits a very high-frequency sound—in the 15,000-hertz range. The Dead Silence call, manufactured by M.A.D. Calls, Inc., produces a sound that aggravates turkeys and makes them "shock-gobble" at ranges of 400 and 500 yards. When that doesn't work he makes a loud, aggressive series of crow calls, which often brings a gobbling response.

"If you can make a turkey gobble to a sound that is not a turkey sound you have a better chance of sneaking in close to him before you start working him with turkey calls," Steve says. "If you use a turkey call to locate a distant gobbler and he starts coming toward you, you lose track of where he is and are too apt to run into him before you're ready."

Like Marc Drury, Steve Stoltz refuses to accept the idea that turkeys are not gobbling. When he can't get a response to normal calling he starts to move, stopping to make a stimulating call in every good-looking place. He moves fast, covers a lot of country, and makes every effort to find that one individual gobbler that is lonesome and ready to respond to calling.

"You just have to keep telling yourself he's out there somewhere and keep looking for him," Steve says. "The longer you go without finding a gobbler that will work, the closer you are getting to the moment when you encounter one that will."

12

LATE-HOUR TURKEY HUNTING

We have all been taught that the classic turkey hunt involves locating a gobbler on his roost the previous evening, then creeping in an hour before dawn and setting up within 100 yards of his tree. You call softly at dawn, trying to entice him to fly down and come to your calls before he goes to his other hens.

Nine times out of 10 it doesn't work.

The gobbler answers all your calls but stays in his tree, demanding that you, along with his other hens, go to him. When a few of his regular girlfriends show up under his tree he drops down, begins breeding the live hens, and eventually wanders off with them—still hollering back every time you call, still demanding that you do what real turkey hens do, which is to run to him.

After a while these unsuccessful dawn hunts begin to wear me down. I get tired of having to sleep on the couch because my wife can't stand my waking her up at 3:30. I get sick of having Ding-Dongs and Dr. Pepper for breakfast because the only place open that early is the gas station. And I find that I don't amount to much in any department after too many four-hour nights.

Over the years I have killed more turkeys in mid- and late morning than I have at the break of dawn. The early-morning, break-of-day hunts are traditional and everybody does them, but ask some veteran turkey hunters when they killed most of their birds, and you may be surprised to hear how many times their success came later in the day.

I realized this at the uncomfortable hour of 3 o'clock one morning when my jangling alarm rousted me from a sweet dream, demanding that it was time to get up and go turkey hunting.

"Today I'm not going to do it," I decided. "I'll go later."

So on a gentle, greening morning in May, I got up at the civilized hour of 7, took my daughter to the school bus, picked up the paper, came home, and ate breakfast. I did a few things in my office until almost 10, then changed into camos, drove a mile or so from home, and slipped into the woods.

By 10:30 I had climbed to an oak flat in a saddle between two mountains. Turkey scratchings were everywhere.

I opened with a series of soft yelps. When they brought no response I switched to a friction call and belted out a sharp run of cutts and cackles. At once a gobbler answered from about a quarter mile away. I ducked through the woods toward him, moving quickly, staying in the thickest cover and avoiding high ground where I might be silhouetted. When I came to a little logging road I set up three decoys, then pulled back about 20 yards and took a seat against the bole of a large red oak. I arranged a few fallen branches around me to break up my outline. Then I popped a diaphragm call into my mouth, slipped my box call out of its pocket, propped my shotgun on my knee with its butt against my shoulder, and checked my watch. It was 10:45.

The gobbler boomed back at the first yelps I stroked from the box call. When I tried him again a couple of minutes later he had halved the distance between us. I laid the box call in the leaves and said something soft and contented with the diaphragm. Then I shut up. I wasn't looking for a conversation with this turkey, I wanted him to be hunting for me.

When I saw him he was about 100 yards out, sneaking toward me, his white head bobbing like a tennis ball, his beard swinging like a pendulum between his legs. When he spotted the decoys he stopped and went into strut. Then he came mincing toward them, tail fanned, beard sprouting, taking tiny steps with menacing moxie, his wings jammed down and quivering with fury.

He went straight to the little jake decoy, the way they always do. He was 17 yards from me when I put the bead on his flaming wattles. It was a just a few minutes past 11.

Lazy man's turkey? Banker's hours hunter? Just plain dumb luck?

Perhaps.

But consider this: I've spent a lot of time with professional turkey hunters, turkey guides, and turkey-hunting videographers. These are hunters who are out there every day of the season, often hunting in 10 or a dozen states each year, starting in Florida in March and winding up the season in New York or New England in late May.

They have told me that the vast majority of the gobblers they call in to the gun or the camera come in after 10 o'clock in the morning. Eleven o'clock until 1 o'clock is the really hot time, they declare.

Late-hour hunts are particularly successful during the period when the gobblers are "henned up" and unresponsive to calls made

Most gobblers are killed later in the morning, not at dawn. After early-morning breeding activity ceases, hens steal away to lay eggs; the gobblers find themselves alone and start seeking company. The author called in this big Eastern gobbler at 11 A.M.

earlier in the day. Hens abandon the gobbler in midmorning and steal off to their nests to lay eggs, finally leaving the gobbler alone. By 10 o'clock or so gobblers are thinking about mating again, but their hens are gone. They begin to wander, looking for company. They may or may not gobble. Often they just sneak around listening for hen sounds, ready to close in on them fast before revealing themselves.

Most of the best video footage of successful turkey hunts is shot late in the morning, I have learned, yet the majority of turkey hunters leave the woods discouraged before these best of all turkey-calling hours arrive. Indeed, successful turkey hunting does not demand the barbarous schedule that most of us believe is absolutely essential.

I still get up early and do the dawn thing when I feel like it, but when other priorities interfere I have discovered that I don't have to give up hunting turkeys altogether—I just go later in the day. And it turns out that later in the day can be the best time of all.

13

PATTERNING
TURKEY
HABITS

The secret to successful turkey hunting is being where the turkey wants to be. Knowing where a gobbler wants to be and when he wants to be there is more important than any turkey-calling skill you can develop.

Danny Pierce, who operates the Rush Creek Guide Service (see pages 64–65) knows more about the patterns of more wild turkey gobblers than any man I know. When I hunted with him in the spring of 1997 Danny knew the daily movement patterns of more than 65 individual longbeards that he had been studying on his more than 20,000 acres of leased hunting land.

"My clients don't have the time to study the habits of individual gobblers," Danny explains. "I figure that's what they're paying me to figure out for them."

All his life Danny has been studying the movements of wildlife and figuring out when and why birds and animals go where they do.

Danny Pierce says the secret to successful turkey hunting is knowing where turkeys want to be. If you are calling from where a gobbler intends to go, the probability that he will respond to your calls goes way, way up.

"I grew up poor," he says. "We didn't have much meat other than what we shot."

Danny told me that when he was a little boy he used to go hunting with his Aunt May, who taught him to study tracks and animal signs so he'd know where to look for game. With her he would sit for hours watching banty chicken hens to see where they went to lay eggs in secret nests that Danny and his aunt could raid for eggs.

Now, as a professional hunting guide, Danny still spends most of his time studying the movements of turkeys, deer, and quail so that he can put his clients into spots he knows are going to produce.

The first day that I hunted with Danny he took me to a little 160- acre lease where he had seen a big longbeard in the company of hens the day before.

"It's only a small place," he admitted. "But it lies between a big timbered draw that's full of turkeys on a ranch that doesn't permit hunting and a natural feeding range on a big cattle operation across the road.

"The birds roost in the draw and then come out to feed on the cattle ranch," he explained. "They funnel through the little piece I've leased."

It was mid-April and the gobblers were all with hens that stayed with them all day. The birds roosted together, fed together, and wandered around together. The hens went where they wanted to go; the gobblers just dragged along behind them and were almost impossible to break away from the flocks.

"We need to be where the hens want to go," Danny said.

The first afternoon we set up beside an old wind-toppled cottonwood just where a little timbered bottom opened up on a vast tallgrass pasture. We put a hen decoy and a little jake decoy 20 yards from our hiding place in a position where they would not be seen until the birds came out of the timber and were almost within gun range.

"When gobblers are just trailing along behind flocks of hens you have to be careful about using decoys," Danny told me. "The hens in those flocks all know each other and they may not want to associate with turkeys that are not part of their regular group. If they see your decoys from a great distance they may avoid them. I like to set the decoys where the hens won't see them until they are pretty close. When the gobbler that's trailing the hen flock sees the decoys up close like that he can sometimes be pulled away from his hens and brought into range."

Late in the afternoon 11 hens and two jakes appeared, but no longbeard was with them. The flock needed little in the way of calling—we were where they wanted to be, and they came into our little corner to loaf before they went into the big timbered draw to roost, just the way Danny knew they would.

We just called softly, reassuring them with purrs and clucks, and soon they were loafing and scratching within a few yards of our decoys and seemed unconcerned about them.

When the birds left us to head for their roosts Danny said, "I don't know why that gobbler wasn't with them. Perhaps a coyote or one of those wild cows ran him off. You can bet he'll join them again in the morning."

We were back in the same location when the eastern sky began to brighten the next morning. It was cold. There was frost on the grass and thin ice on the puddles, but the clear sky promised a bright sun and welcome warmth later on.

Half an hour before sunrise the gobblers in the big timbered draw began to sound off. We could identify at least eight separate gobblers; there were probably more that were remaining silent, and more still beyond the limit of our hearing. On the open range coyotes sang and yammered, celebrating the dawn.

"It won't be long now," Danny whispered. "When they fly down they'll probably go silent for a while while the gobblers breed their hens. After a while the hens will wander out to feed, and the gobblers will follow where they go. We'll just sit here and wait for them. Don't call much — just enough to let the gobbler know there's a hen here."

We heard birds fly down a few hundred yards away. As Danny had predicted the gobbling soon stopped, and for an hour or so we heard little from the turkeys. Every 10 minutes or so I stroked some pretty yelps from a box call, but I did nothing aggressive that might make the hen flock decide to avoid our little piece of woods.

"I saw them here yesterday at 10 o'clock, and the longbeard was with them," Danny assured me. "I don't know how long they'd been here when I saw them, but I'm willing to bet he'll be here by 10 o'clock this morning."

By 8 o'clock I was cold, and there had been no response to my calls. Without Danny's certain knowledge of the habits of this flock of turkeys I doubt I would have waited until 10 o'clock. Without his confidence in this place I think I would have gotten fidgety, lost patience, and probably decided to move and look for turkeys I could see or hear someplace else.

"Stay where you are," Danny said. "He'll come here by 10."

I continued to issue encouraging invitations with the box call at regular intervals, but there were no answering gobbles.

Then, at 9:45, two hens appeared and strolled into the trees near us. I called to them softly; they looked over at the decoys, apparently unconcerned. They were doing their own thing, not being led by my calls, but neither were they put off by them.

At 9:55 Marc Scroggins, who was behind me filming this hunt with a video camera, whispered, "I just heard one gobble. Where was it?"

We all listened intently, and then it came again, a distant chant, coming not from the big timbered draw from which the hens emerged but from the open range behind us, where the hen flock had appeared the evening before.

I yelped loudly now with the box call to reach out to the gobbler. He boomed back at me from the open range.

"I see him," Marc whispered. "He's crossing that pasture toward the bluff on the east about 300 yards away."

I turned my head to peek, and then I could see him, too. He was a big bird, and he was hurrying across the open pasture on an angle toward us that would briefly put him behind the cover of the eastern bluff.

"When he disappears we'll have to change positions," Marc said. "We need to get the gun out front and the camera behind you."

When the bird disappeared we clambered to exchange positions. No sooner had we accomplished the flip when the bird reappeared, now only 100 yards away.

Expecting the hen flock to approach from the south and perhaps not come all the way to our decoys, we had placed them slightly behind and off to the side of our shooting position. This way a gobbler coming from the south would come into our gun range when he was still about 40 yards from the decoys.

But now the tables were turned. The gobbler was coming from the north and would see the decoys from a long distance away.

"He's alone," Danny whispered. "He expects to meet his hens here. He'll come all the way in to the decoys, so don't shoot too soon."

This gobbler came in like he was on a rope. He stopped and blew up into a full strut when he saw the decoys; we could hear him drumming as he continued to step toward us. He would take a normal step or two then scoot forward with tiny, mincing steps. His head was flashing red, white, and blue; his fully fanned tail caught the bright morning sunshine; his black body feathers radiated iridescent bronze, copper, blue, and green.

He stopped once when he came to a log on the ground under a big cottonwood tree, but Marc spoke to him softly with crooning notes from a diaphragm call, and the big bird crossed over the log and came marching into sure killing range.

I followed his progress with the bead of my old double-barreled turkey gun on his blazing red wattles. When he stepped past the decoys at a range of 12 yards Marc whispered, "Now," and I squeezed the rear trigger.

He was an old bird with 1¼-inch spurs; a large patch of his breast feathers had been rubbed away by his breeding activities. The tips of his primary wing feathers were broken off and squared from having been driven into the sandy soil and dragged as he strutted.

"He's probably four years old," Danny said. "He's a dominant bird that has done plenty of breeding and accomplished his life's purpose. By the day after tomorrow another old gobbler will be trying to hook up with these hens, and they'll meet him at this very spot. If we come back two days from now, we'll kill us another big old bird, you wait and see."

Danny's knowledge of the birds on his hunting land had me convinced that whatever he predicted was sure to pan out, so two days later we were back in the same place with the decoys in the same position. When we crawled up against that big old fallen cottonwood tree, listened to the chorus of gobbling begin again in the big draw, and heard the coyotes sing their tribute to the dawning of another day, I was not just hopeful that a bird would show up but confident that we were keeping an appointment with a tom that expected to find hens waiting exactly where our decoys now stood. He would be listening for our calls.

This time it didn't take until 10 o'clock.

A turkey began gobbling before daylight from a tree not more than 200 yards away. When I answered with some sleepy tree yelps he boomed back at me. I gave him a few more soft yelps to make sure he knew exactly where I waited, then put the call down.

"Don't call him much while he's still in his tree or he'll just wait there for you to come to him," Danny said. "Wait until he's on the ground and then invite him to come on over."

I had brought along the feathered joint of a wing from the turkey I had killed here two days earlier; 10 minutes after my last call I took it out and beat it against my leg, imitating the sound of a turkey flying down from his roost. Then I made a few soft yelps and put the wing away.

The turkey double-gobbled in response, but now I went silent.

Soon we heard a continuous clatter that lasted several seconds as turkeys down the length of the big timbered draw flew from their roosts. When the clamor subsided I stroked out a run of loud yelps and clucks to let the nearby gobbler know that a hen was still here and waiting.

We heard him fly down now, and when he was on the ground he gobbled. In the next half hour I suppose he gobbled 50 or 60 times, all the time moving closer. He hung up for a long time in timber just across the road about 100 yards from where we hid, demanding that the hen he heard go to him, but when I continued to answer with clucks and occasional aggressive cutts he became frustrated. Soon we saw him step into the road, cross it, and duck down into the timber on our side.

"We've got him now," Danny whispered. "Just give him some soft purrs and clucks and then get your gun ready."

We could see the gobbler walking toward us slowly through the timber, stopping every few steps to look things over. When he moved into the open he was 50 yards away, and from there he saw the decoys. I clucked twice and laid the box call on the ground.

The gobbler started walking toward the decoys. Then he stopped and went into full strut. We heard him drum. He slicked and long-necked the decoys. I think it was at that moment that he noticed the red head and jutting little beard, and recognized the jake decoy as competition for the hen that stood beside it.

The gobbler stuck his head straight out and began to trot toward the decoys. His head went from red to white and now he was coming at a dead run. I had my gun up with the bead on his neck as he ran in. When he passed the last bush and was streaking across the clearing toward the decoys that stood behind us and slightly to the side. I whispered sharply to Marc, "Stop him!"

Marc fired off three sharp cutts with the diaphragm call he had ready in his mouth. The big bird slammed to a stop and blew up in full strut with all his colors flashing, his tail fanned, and his wings jammed into the ground 10 yards in front of us.

"Take him," Marc whispered. "He's filling my lens."

That was a three-year-old, 19-pound gobbler with 1-inch spurs and a 9-inch beard, and once again we had connected because of Danny's knowledge of his birds' movement patterns. He knew where the turkeys wanted to be and put us there before they showed up.

"Luck happens when preparedness meets opportunity," Danny says. "When you know where the birds want to be you're pretty well prepared."

14

SIT WHERE YOU CAN SEE

One of the most important factors in successful turkey hunting is where and how you sit. A poor position binds you up and cramps you from covering certain directions with your gun; worse, when you can't see well you are tempted to move around, twisting your head this way and that—and this kind of movement is exactly what turkeys are sure to spot.

When you choose a place to stop and call, look for a flat spot with a large tree, stump, or rock to lean back against. Choose a place that gives a clear view to the front and sides extending for at least shotgun range, and do not cramp yourself up against any object that will prevent you from swiveling on your seat in order to cover more area off your shooting shoulder should the bird come from that side.

Sit where you are protected from behind, in a place that gives clear visibility to the front and sides for at least shotgun range. Don't cramp yourself up against any object that will prevent you from swiveling on your seat to cover more area comfortably.

Turkeys have a way of coming from the side you least expect them to. Suppose you've set up hearing a bird directly in front of you; if you have the kind of luck that makes you a regular winner in the Irish Sweepstakes, he'll come straight to you as if you were pulling him in on a rope. Of course most of us don't have that kind of luck, and there's no telling how a turkey will approach our calls.

Sometimes his approach will be influenced by terrain or obstacles that he must go around. But a turkey's instinctive wariness makes it unlikely that he will come straight in even under the best of conditions. Often a gobbler will circle, keeping just out of view, stopping to spit and drum, demanding that the hen he hears go to him, and refusing to reveal himself.

"I've come this far," the tom is saying to the hen he hears but cannot see. "Now you come to me."

When no hen appears the tom may circle to look things over from a higher elevation. Longspurs didn't grow old by making mistakes. They have all the time in the world and are usually unwilling to rush into an unnatural situation in which a hen they cannot see refuses to show herself.

If you're seated in a cramped position from which you can't see in all directions the chances that the turkey will appear in your restricted shooting zone get mighty slim.

I blew it on a big Merriam one time in the Pine Ridge country of northwestern Nebraska because I sat down wrong.

I chose the place because it was so comfortable. A big old ponderosa pine log lay on the ground with the curve of its rotted root structure making a nice rounded backrest. Sitting there, facing the length of the log, I could cover everything to my left and straight out in front, but the log prevented me from swinging to my right.

I didn't think that would matter. There was nothing behind me but open ground, and the terrain to my right was very steep. I was facing a long timbered draw with a relatively gentle slope. If a bird came I was sure he would come from this direction. So sure, in fact, that I set my decoys uphill and slightly to the right of my comfortable seat; my idea was that they would be seen by the gobbler as he came up through the timber, and that he would walk right across my most comfortable shooting zone at no more than 25 yards as he approached them.

It was a great scenario, but I learned that it's a mistake to think you know exactly what a turkey will do. It's like Mike Morton says, "They're turkeys—you never know what the bastards are going to do."

When the turkey answered my call he was just where I had expected him to be, straight down the draw. Ten minutes later he had halved the distance to me, and he was still coming as I'd planned, like he was being towed to me.

He gobbled back each time I gave him the old box call's promise of extravagant pleasure. When I went quiet and refused to answer his demands that I run to meet him, he came closer.

But just at the point where he should have stepped into view he hung up.

I could hear him spit and drum just over the edge of a bulge in the terrain that prevented me from seeing him. He was in the cover of a little patch of thick growth from which he could very well be periscoping my position without my seeing him.

I stayed absolutely still and did not call back when he gobbled. I wanted him to search for me now. No more conversation back and forth.

I was positive that the bird would next see the decoys, show himself, and begin his advance across my shooting zone. That's what I would have done, had I been the turkey. Trouble was, I wasn't.

He never quite stepped into a position from which he could see the decoys. Instead he began to circle to the right, staying behind cover and over the edge of the terrain so that he couldn't be seen. In the course of the next hour the bird continued to boom his demands that the hen he heard come over the hill and show herself.

Eventually he began to move around the top of the rise. The next time I heard him he gobbled from behind me. He was on the open ground now, approaching from my rear, yet he was still in a position from which the terrain hid his view of the decoys.

He was hunting me now, finally closing in on the precise location from which he had heard my calls, but he was coming from the one direction I couldn't cover with my gun without swiveling: My comfortable seat in the curve of the log-and-root structure prevented me from turning to my right without getting up.

While he was still hidden from view by the terrain I swiveled as far as I could to my right and got my gun up over the log. I was screwed into a cramped position from which there was no relief.

Just then he gobbled again, not 30 yards behind me and to my right. Out of the corner of my eye I saw the tips of his fanned tail feathers coming up over the ridge — exactly at the angle from which I could swing my gun no farther to the right.

He was a grand sight. His long Merriam tail with its cream-colored rim looked like a cartwheel and, as he stepped forward in full strut, now finally focused on the decoys, he showed himself fully. His colors blazed in the sunlight and it seemed he had a beard so long he had to kick it out of the way to take a step.

I was just able to cover him by forcing my gun to its most extreme right-hand position as I bound myself up against the log. When I got the bead on his wattles I fired.

But this bird didn't react to the shot as I'd planned. Instead he ducked back over the edge of the terrain. When I next saw him he was flying across the steep draw from which he'd come. I ran out and searched the ground for feathers but found none. I had missed him clean.

Disgusted with my shooting performance after such a long and challenging bout of calling, I sat down again in my shooting position and re-created the shot.

"I was right like this, and he was right there," I told myself as I raised my gun. . . . And then I looked down my gun barrel.

In that cramped position I could not get my face all the way down on the stock. My gun was elevated like a ramp. I had put the bead on the turkey's neck, but I had not been looking flat down the barrel. By failing to mount my gun correctly I had shot at least a foot over the head of the finest Merriam turkey I have ever seen.

So much for comfortable seating. If I'd sat against the trunk of any of the ponderosas that surrounded me I could have swiveled as the bird moved right out of sight, and had a comfortable shot when he finally reappeared from the direction where I'd least expected him.

You're better off sitting in the open and staying still than hiding yourself in thick cover from which your shooting zone is restricted.

"You're better off sitting in the open and staying still than you are to have a comfortable seat with good cover from which your shooting zone is restricted," Danny Pierce told me once when I was hunting Rio Grande turkeys with him in Texas. "The most important thing is to sit in a position that gives you the least-restricted shooting zone."

I had good reason to honor this advice. On a previous trip to Nebraska I had also spotted a pair of longbeards with a bunch of hens way out in an open pasture. There was no way I could approach the birds, so I just watched them from behind a tree along the edge of the forest. At about 10 o'clock the group started drifting toward the low end of the pasture.

I dropped back into the trees and hurried around to that side. I selected a low saddle at the edge of the forest as a likely place for the birds to exit from the pasture and committed myself to making my stand there.

The birds were still about 200 yards from the forest edge, and I was able to belly out through tallgrass and place three decoys in a spot where they could easily be seen. Then I crawled back through the grass, entered the forest, and sat back against a big ponderosa pine about four trees back into the woods.

That was my mistake.

From my seat inside the tree line I could see the decoys, but a slight rise in the terrain between us prevented me from seeing beyond them. That didn't bother me at the time because I expected the gobblers to come all the way to the decoys and offer a good close-range shot as soon as they appeared.

I made a brief run of calls, and both gobblers boomed back at me.

"I'm in business," I told myself. But after that initial response the gobblers went silent. I clucked and purred and yelped a little from time to time, but got no response. I was sure that the birds had seen the decoys, however, and were coming in quietly. I didn't want to call too much if they were in a silent mood.

The next half hour was torture. I couldn't see a thing. Were they coming? Were they drifting away? All my impulses told me to rise up and peek, but I knew that could be my undoing, so I stayed put and waited.

When I finally saw the turkeys they were not where I had expected them to be. Instead of appearing close to the decoy set the birds were avoiding it and moving from the pasture into the forest about 35 yards to my right. I saw three hens cross into the woods. Then I caught sight of a gobbler with his tail half fanned, following the hens. He was crossing in a low spot, and I could only see the top of his back and tail. I couldn't see his chest to check his beard length, and in his half-strut position it was impossible for me to check the fullness of his fan. Still, both of the gobblers I had seen with this bunch were longbeards, so when his big red head reappeared, I had my gun up. As he stepped into an open spot, still in a half strut, I pulled the bead down onto his wattles and fired.

Imagine my surprise when, upon my shot, two longbeards erupted into flight from a position I could not see just beyond the decoys. They had come to the decoys after all and been strutting only a few yards beyond them—just out of my sight. Because I'd been unable to see them, I killed what I was ashamed to discover was a jake that I had not even realized was traveling with the group.

So much for a shooting position hidden back in the woods. If I had instead taken my seat against one of the trees on the front edge of the forest I could have seen the birds approaching, would have recognized the jake for what he was, and would have seen that the two longbeards were going to the decoys even though the hens and the jake chose to avoid them and skirt the edges of the set.

As Danny Pierce told me, "Sit where you can see—but sit still."

THE TURKEY LOUNGER

In order to sit still, you have to be comfortable.

The most comfortable seat I have found is the Turkey Lounger, a product that I consider the ultimate turkey-hunting vest.

It features a built-in padded backrest with an internal frame that offers full back support, and a padded waterproof seat with adjustable side straps that folds down from inside the vest while you're wearing it, enabling you to sit comfortably anywhere.

The vest also has a special zippered box call pocket, plus three more large pockets for other calls and equipment. An oversize, waterproof game pouch with quick-release buckles provides plenty of room for carrying both collapsible decoys and a large turkey.

The Turkey Lounger is available with a lifetime guarantee in

The Turkey Lounger is a turkey-hunting vest with lots of pockets and a unique built-in seat and backrest that enable you to sit comfortably for long periods of time just about anywhere.

two popular camouflage patterns from Bucklick Creek, 147 Samson Lane, New Haven, MO 63068 (1-800-351-0086). (A safety orange model with different pocket arrangements is available for big-game hunters.)

HUNTING TURKEYS FROM A BLIND

For some reason few turkey hunters build blinds for turkey hunting. Yet there are certain places in the turkey woods that stand out as ideal spots to set up for calling and displaying decoys. You might find it advantageous to make comfortable hiding places in several such spots, using them when turkeys are not gobbling and you have no way of knowing where the birds are.

I have several turkey blinds scattered around in the woods I hunt most often. They are located at places where I have successfully called in gobblers or in particularly heavily used feeding areas where I expect turkeys to go regularly.

The blinds don't amount to much—just a low arrangement of branches on the ground around a comfortable place to sit against a big tree or stump. I usually clip some leafy branches and stick them in among the dry branches that I pile up around the place where I sit.

I make sure that the blind does not interfere with my view or ability to raise my gun. Generally these blinds are no more than 24 inches high. I add just enough cover to allow me to move my hands without being seen; this way I can use hand calls even when a turkey is in sight. I also try to arrange a solid support, where I can lean my shotgun within easy reach.

In some cases I make the blind in a circle shape around a tree so that I can move around the tree to face the direction from which the turkey is approaching. I keep the ground within the blind free of noisy debris so I can move quietly.

To qualify as a prospective blind location a spot must meet three requirements: It must be in a place that shows signs of heavy recent turkey use; it must offer an open view of the surrounding woods; and there must be a prominent location within 20 yards from which decoys can easily be seen from a good distance.

I am convinced that spots that meet these requirements are where I want to be when I can't find a bird gobbling anyplace else. Just as deer hunters have particular places where they go regularly to intercept deer, turkey hunters can benefit by having previously chosen the best places from which to call turkeys.

15

THE LAW OF AVERAGES

The gobblers were henned up and neither my companion nor I had been able to get a bird to play for the past two days. I mentioned that we needed a change of luck.

"When a gobbler hasn't shown up yet, one's fixin' to."

That was Jim Clay's advice one April morning as we were getting ready to go our separate ways in the northern Virginia turkey woods. It was his southern way of making a point that is worth remembering whenever you're hunting—the longer you go without seeing anything, the closer you're getting to the moment when your quarry will appear. So you've got to stay ready every moment and never stop expecting a bird to appear.

Hunting any wary game is mostly a matter of not seeing anything while putting in time in an area that has good prospects. The minute you let your guard down, watch out—that's just when your bird, or your buck, will show up.

How many times have you come to the conclusion that nothing is going to happen and stood up, only to have a gobbler fly or run off that you never knew was there?

Jim and I were hunting that morning on a pretty little abandoned farmstead. No one lived in the old house anymore, and the weathered barn was sagging. The pastures and fields were just greening up, and the redbud was in bloom. A quick little stream meandered through the bottomland meadow.

The evening before had been windy and we hadn't been able to hear a gobbler go to roost. Still, we were in good turkey country, and we knew gobblers had been roosting nearby.

I set my three decoys—two hens and a little standing jake—along the meadow's edge where they would be visible to any bird that came within 100 yards of where I hid myself, at the base of a fallen tree 20 yards back into the timber from the edge.

At dawn three gobblers sounded off. One was behind me on a low pine ridge. Another was across the creek in the sycamore bottom, and the third bird was farther away on the shoulder of a hardwood hill downstream along the creek, where Jim had gone.

The three birds gobbled mightily from their roosting trees; the one on the ridge behind me boomed back answers to my soft tree yelps. When I stroked a fly-down cackle and some aggressive cutts from my box call the gobbler shook the ground with his demand that I go to him. But as time passed and his insistent gobbles moved away along the ridge, it became clear that he had hens with him and was not going to come to me.

I spent the next hour following that bird and coaxing him, but he wouldn't come. By 9 o'clock he had wandered onto a farm where we lacked permission to hunt, so I gave up on him.

Discouraged, I turned back and moved back toward the creek

to see if I could pick up with one of the other turkeys I'd heard at daybreak.

When I got back to the meadow I saw Jim coming down off the ridge above the farm. He spotted me and beckoned me to come over.

"I've got a bird that wants to play," he told me. "He'll come toward me but he won't come far enough to see the decoys. I figure we can sneak in close to him and set the decoys and leave you watching them. Then I'll move back and call from farther away. If he comes toward me as I move away, he ought to come to where he can see the decoys. Then you can cluck him in."

Very quietly we went back to a fork in a little logging road at the end of a ridge about 150 yards from where Jim had last heard the gobbler.

"I'll just make one call to locate him," Jim said.

He took out a crow call. No sooner had he begun to scream a raucous series than the turkey shock-gobbled back at him from no more than 50 yards away. He was right on top of us—so close that we couldn't move. Together we flattened ourselves against the edge of a big rock outcropping that bordered the roadway and tried to blend in. The bird sounded so close that we were afraid even to try to put the decoys out.

I scrunched into a position that would give me a shot up the logging road if the bird came into it; Jim was positioned to cover the other direction in case the bird circled us and came from that side. Jim shrugged his shoulders and rolled his eyes upward toward the bird in a sign of hopeful resignation.

Then he made three soft yelps with his mouth call. The gobbler blasted back at him with a double gobble and then gobbled again. He was even closer now, but we couldn't see above the rock outcropping, and he hadn't moved down toward the roadway.

"He's hot," Jim whispered. "Watch out."

Jim made a soft cluck then turned his head away and made another, attempting to make it sound as if the hen was moving away. That brought a gobble that made the hairs tingle on my neck. The bird was directly above us now and very close.

Jim went silent, trying to make the gobbler hunt for him rather than giving the impression that the gobbler could expect the hen to move to him. When the bird gobbled again he had moved back along the ridge away from us.

Hoping that the bird was going to circle the rock outcropping and come down to our level, where we could see him, Jim let him go and did not call back.

Minutes passed. The bird did not show up in the road. Then he gobbled again from his original position farther out along the ridge.

With all this gobbling going on it would be only a matter of time before the gobbler called in a hen; I began to worry that, once again, we were about to lose a gobbler to live competition. When the

When a gobbler that has been answering your calls suddenly goes silent don't make the mistake of thinking he has lost interest. It's more likely that he's sneaking in on you and is about to appear in view.

bird remained silent for several more minutes and still did not show up in the roadway I began to suspect that a live hen may already have gone to him.

When a gobbler goes silent you never know whether he has moved off or is coming to you, but you should always play it safe and assume he is coming in.

Trying once more to locate the bird Jim made a little run of yelps with an insistent series of cutts at the end. There was no answer.

I was now convinced that the gobbler had called in a hen and was drifting away with her. After several more minutes passed and there was still no sound from the gobbler, I mentally wrote this bird off and began to hope for better luck next time.

Right then I should have reminded myself of Jim's early-morning caution: "When no bird shows up, one's fixin' to." I should have stayed still.

But we had been crouched in uncomfortable positions for more than 40 minutes, and I was cramped and sore. Convinced that the gobbler was gone, I separated my shoulders from the ledge and began to turn toward Jim.

That was my undoing.

My slight movement was a classic mistake. Before I finished turning the sky exploded with the *wowf-wowf-wowf* of big wings grabbing air. Not 10 yards above me the gobbler was aloft, his long beard dangling as he flushed through the treetops from the top of the very ledge under which Jim and I had been hiding.

Either of us could have shot the gobbler in the air if we'd thought of it, but we jut sat there in a catatonic state of mixed terror and open-mouthed amazement.

"He was standing right above us, watching us all the time," Jim groaned. "He sneaked in on top of us and stood there looking for that hen he kept hearing. Why didn't one of us think to look up?"

The longer you go without having a gobbler come to your calls, the closer you are to the moment when one is going to show up. You must stay ready and never stop expecting a bird to appear.

When a bird goes silent you've got to believe that he's coming in. The longer you go without seeing a bird, the closer you're getting to the time when one is going to come in. It's the same basic law of averages you learned in school.

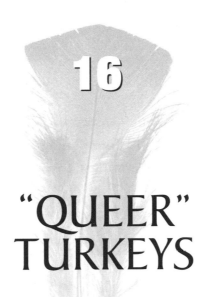

16

"QUEER" TURKEYS

I was in northern Missouri one April morning with Don Shipp, the 1997 World Turkey Calling Champion, and we figured we could hear 18 different gobblers sounding off at dawn. There were 8 within what Don considered decent calling distance and 10 more strung out in the distance. As that bright spring morning broke I figured we were in for sure action.

Don plied the air with the kind of absolutely realistic, plaintive calls that had won him the world championship, but the turkeys turned a deaf ear. He couldn't buy an answer. The turkeys had gobbled on their limbs, but once they hit the ground it was as if they'd gone into holes. The woods were silent.

"You sure sounded good," I offered.

"Thanks, but this time we're up against the toughest judges of all, real wild turkeys," Don replied. "Sometimes you can't say anything they want to hear."

"They must be queer," I said. "You sounded like the most lovesick hen turkey I can imagine."

"They're queer all right. They've been like this around here a lot this season," Don said. "It's like they don't care for hen turkeys."

A week later I was in Virginia hunting with Jim Clay. We were having the same kind of day: a little bit of gobbling in the distance at dawn, then nothing. We spent the entire morning walking slowly through the best-looking turkey woods I have ever seen. Turkey sign was everywhere. It seemed there was no ground that turkeys had not

scratched. We found tracks in every damp spot and lots of droppings scattered about.

Jim was trying everything he knew to make a turkey gobble, but he got no answers. He stroked seductive notes from a tube call, cutt with a raspy box call, yelped with diaphragm call, purred and clucked with a slate call, and sucked a mellow series of notes from a wing-bone call, but the turkeys did not care.

"It's been like this a lot this year," Jim said. "Turkeys aren't acting like they're supposed to."

"Same thing where I

Don Shipp believes that in areas where turkey populations have saturated the available habitat, a significant number of gobblers lose the desire to mate with hens and therefore don't bother answering seductive hen calls.

was in Missouri last week," I replied. "Don Shipp thinks turkeys are turning queer."

"There's something to that," Jim said. He was serious. "They probably are turning queer."

Then he explained. "In nature wildlife sexual behavior is influenced by population dynamics," Jim said. "When populations approach the limit that the area can support, animals and birds begin to breed at older ages, have fewer offspring, and fewer individuals actually mate. You have increasing numbers of males and females that do not mate. The result is a static population that is no longer growing.

"In this region the turkey population is at total saturation," Jim went on. "The biologists say that the turkey population here is at its peak. So the flocks are made up of fewer breeding birds, and a greater proportion of the flock is made up of the nonreproductive individuals that have no interest in mating and are not responsive to mating calls."

Dominant gobblers are often accompanied by mature male turkeys that do not attempt to mate with hens. These nonbreeding companion turkeys may gobble in answer to hen calls, but are not likely to seek out hens they hear calling.

"Queer turkeys," I deducted.

"That's right," Jim said. "One gobbler in each flock does all the breeding, but there will often be other gobblers present that watch and masturbate but never attempt to breed a hen. The gobblers that want to breed already have all the hens they want with them, so they're often not responsive to calls either."

"What's a hunter supposed to do in a situation like this?" I asked.

"Just what we're doing," Jim said. "Move through the woods slowly and quietly, stopping to call every so often until you get a response. It may take days before you come into range of a turkey that is interested in breeding and is not already with a harem, but it will happen eventually.

"Once the peak of breeding activity passes and hens begin to stay on their nests incubating eggs, they want nothing to do with other turkeys," he continued. "That's when hunting usually gets good again. The dominant breeding males that can't find their hens and go looking for them are vulnerable. Gobbling activity increases, and those birds that are looking for hens will come to a call.

"Every time you take a breeding bird out of the flock you make room for another male turkey to become a breeder," Jim explained. "It's just nature's way of limiting population numbers by adjusting the behavior of individuals. The pecking order. Survival of the fittest."

17

STALKING
WILD
TURKEYS

Whatever wild turkeys lack in the ability to reason is more than made up for by an instinctive wariness that makes them distrust anything unusual. Turkeys live in a state of constant apprehension. Anything that moves is cause for alarm until it is identified as something known to be safe—and then the turkeys worry about what may happen next. Blessed with binocular, wraparound vision that enables them to see everything scary in all but a narrow band directly behind their heads, turkeys continually fuel their paranoia.

That is why it's usually easier to call a turkey to you than it is to sneak up on him.

Nevertheless, when a gobbler has hens with him and refuses to investigate your calls, the temptation to stalk the bird sometimes becomes overpowering.

That happened to me one rainy day in Missouri.

Marc Drury and I had spotted a big gobbler strutting in the middle of a long hay field. We could see two hens with him and there may have been more. There was a stock pond with brushy cover around it about 200 yards from the birds; we figured that we could use the terrain to our advantage and get to the stock pond without being seen. That would put us within calling range of the bird.

We circled around to approach the stock pond from the far side. Once we were within the cover we made our way to the edge that faced the birds.

Rising slowly behind a tree, Marc rolled one eye around the trunk and took a peek.

"They're still there," he said. "They haven't moved."

I rose up behind Marc and peeked over his shoulder. The gobbler was in full strut, his tail fanned like a wagon wheel. The hens were not in sight.

As I've mentioned before, it's very difficult to call a gobbler out of an open field to the edge of cover. He usually just anchors himself on safe ground and demands that the hen he hears go to him.

Marc gave it a try anyway. He started with a run of soft, plaintive yelps that brought an immediate rousing response. More yelps mixed with sharp cutts brought demanding gobbles every time, but we could still see the old bird all puffed up and fanned out in the exact spot where we'd first spotted him.

After half an hour of frustration Marc said, "Let's crawl on him."

The rain had stopped but now a strong wind was blowing across the hay field, lashing the tallgrass and making swishing noises that would cover the sounds of our approach.

It was a Marine-style crawl on bellies and elbows, and we were instantly soaked by the rain-wet grass. Faces to the ground and rumps down, we more or less swam through the grass toward the bird. We found a slight depression in the ground and stayed within it, taking advantage of a nearby rise to hide us from the gobbler. We could not afford to raise our heads to judge our distance from the bird but just crawled on, mentally calculating our advance.

After what seemed like about the right distance Marc motioned for me to keep my head down while he inched his masked face upward very slightly.

I saw him begin to raise his head then freeze. Slowly he lowered his face to the ground again and turned to me wide eyed. With a finger beside his face he pointed.

"Fifteen yards," he whispered. "You take him."

I brought the gun up beside me and slowly rolled onto my side to get into a shooting position. Then I got one elbow under me for support and began to raise my head.

At first I could see nothing—the bird had his head down. Then he lifted it for a periscope view, and I could see it glowing red through the haze of wind-lashed grass. When he lowered it again I brought the gun to my shoulder and waited for the next moment, when his head would reappear.

It was a terribly uncomfortable position. The weight of the gun unbalanced me and my stomach muscles were tight from the effort to keep myself from slumping forward. Seconds passed and my arms began to shake.

Then his head came up again, red as a rose and no more than 15 yards away.

I pushed the bead toward his head and squeezed off the shot.

The gun roared and the big bird burst into the air at the same instant. By the time I had summoned my cramped muscles and staggered to my feet the gobbler was out of range, hurtling downwind. The two hens that were with him were also in the air, beating it downwind.

"You missed him!" Marc wailed. "We just pulled off the most impossible sneak and you missed him.

"You're a hell of a stalker, but you can't shoot worth a damn," he went on, rubbing it in. "You sure can scare 'em, though. . . ."

18

WHY
WE MISS
TURKEYS

Missing a turkey at close range with a shotgun is one of life's most embarrassing events, yet it happens a lot more frequently than you may think.

Sure, a turkey is as big as a barrel and will probably be standing still or walking slowly, but that doesn't matter a bit—your target is just his head and neck, and loading that small area with shot is like trying to center your pattern on an apple with a catalpa bean dangling beneath it. It's a tiny target.

We sometimes miss that tiny target because we're not accustomed to aiming shotguns. Shotguns are designed to be pointed ahead of moving targets, not aimed at targets that are standing still. For this reason many shotguns are even designed to shoot a bit high. This helps if your target is a rising bird, but it puts the shot right over a turkey's head when he's standing still at close range.

Hunters often miss turkeys at close range because they fail to get their heads all the way down on the stock, causing the gun to shoot high. This hunter has added rifle sights to his shotgun to remind him to get his head down and aim accurately.

A turkey gun is a very specialized shotgun. It is imperative that you make whatever adjustments may be necessary to make your shot pattern center exactly where you aim.

For this reason the veteran turkey hunters I know all have some sort of sights on their turkey guns. Some have mounted adjustable rifle sights on the rib. This permits them to adjust their sights until their shot pattern is centered dead on target. Others use the battery-powered Aim-Point sight, which accomplishes the same thing and also allows the shooter to fire with his head in a raised position. Once the Aim-Point sight has been adjusted properly the shot pattern will go exactly where the red spot in the center of the sight indicates, regardless of the shooter's head position.

Some hunters use low-powered telescopic sights to achieve the same advantage, adjusting the crosshairs to the center of the pattern.

This shotgun is equipped with an Aim-Point sight in which a battery-powered red dot inside the scope is adjusted to the center of the shotgun's proved shot pattern. Regardless of how the gun is held, the shot will go where the red dot indicates.

Another useful sight for turkey hunting is this Weaver Quick-Point, which uses an adjustable fiber-optic red dot. When the red dot has been adjusted to the center of the gun's pellet pattern, the load will center where the red dot indicates, no matter how you hold the gun.

All have taken the time to sight in their turkey gun, just as a rifle is sighted in, and make whatever adjustments are necessary to ensure that the shot pattern centers at the point of aim.

I recently added a pair of Tru-Glo fiber-optic sights to my turkey gun, and I must agree that they do make me remember to get my face down on the stock, and to line up the sights before I shoot. The fiber-optic, light-gathering beads glow brightly; you really cannot look down a barrel that has them without being reminded to line the sights up.

Shooting with a raised head is the classic reason why we miss turkeys.

It's almost automatic to raise your head and peek at the turkey as he approaches. Still, this is just when you ought to be getting your cheek right down on the stock and lining up the sights on the turkey's wattles.

Part of the problem is the hats we wear. Long-billed baseball-style hunting caps are fine if you remember to position them so that the bill does not interfere with your view when you lower your face to the stock and try to line the sights up on the turkey. If the hat's bill is low, however, you will have to tilt your head back in order to see; your sight picture will then be significantly skewed.

I shot clean over a turkey's head one time in Missouri because I didn't have a clear view of the bird; I had my head up, watching his approach and waiting for his head to appear in an opening. When he did come into the open at about 20 yards I swung the bead to cover his head and fired before remembering to get my face down on the stock. He disappeared in an instant, wiser and unscathed.

That's why it's important to remember that your target should be the turkey's neck, not his head. Aim at the base of the wattles, right where the bunched red flesh of the neck joins the black feathers. A charge of shot centered on the wattles will cover the head as well, but half of a charge aimed at the bird's head will fly high even if your aim is true; the entire charge may go high if you have not mounted your shotgun perfectly.

The expert turkey hunters I know have all missed turkeys at one time or another. Some have missed more than they like to admit. The reason that they all have mounted some sort of adjustable sights on their turkey guns is not that they are gadget freaks. They have added special sights because they identified why they missed birds and did what they could to remedy the situation.

19

THE RIGHT
TURKEY GUN

I f you're willing to wait and take only shots at very close range, the right turkey gun for you is any full-choked, 12-gauge shotgun that fits you well and gives you pleasure. It does not have to be a "long-range" gun, for when everything goes right turkey hunting is not a long-range sport; it requires only a shotgun that will throw a devastating pattern at 25 yards.

However, if you have any doubts about your ability to become a purist who is willing to let birds at more than 25 yards walk, you should equip your turkey gun with a special "turkey choke" that will fill a pie plate with shot at 40 yards.

A normal full choke is designed to hit a flying bird when the entire bird is the target. To make that possible it is designed to put the maximum number of pellets in a 30-inch circle at 40 yards.

Turkey hunting is not supposed to be a long-range sport. If you can call effectively and sit still and wait for a close shot, any gun that throws a devastating pattern at 25 yards is sufficient.

Although turkeys are the largest of gamebirds, your target here is not the entire bird but only the head and neck. For turkey hunting, then, you want a choke that will put the maximum number of pellets in a 10-inch circle at 40 yards.

Proper fit is often overlooked by turkey hunters, who typically buy a gun off the rack and shoot it as is. Yet a gun with a stock that has been fitted to your individual physique will shoot more accurately for you, will come up much more smoothly, and will be right on target every time when you shoulder the gun and sight down the barrel.

Having your shotgun fitted to you is a quick process and can be relatively inexpensive. It will make your gun much more pleasurable to shoot.

Your gunsmith or stock maker will have you snap your unloaded gun to your shoulder and hold that position. He'll sight down the barrel from the muzzle end back to your eye to determine whether the gun will shoot to the left or right, or high or low, when fired from that position. He'll probably repeat this exercise several times to make sure that you consistently hold the gun in the same position.

He then can steam the stock until it becomes pliable and, according to his findings, use a jig to bend the stock left, right, up, or down to compensate for your individual idiosyncrasies. He may also either shorten or lengthen the stock to make it fit you so well that you can snap it to your shoulder and find the bead automatically on your target every time without having to change your aim or make any adjustments.

In some cases the gunsmith may add weight to the stock by drilling a hole under the butt cap and filling it with lead, or lighten it by drilling and removing some wood. These operations change the balance of the gun so that it becomes faster pointing and either more or less muzzle heavy, according to your preference.

Recently there has been a rush to develop "turkey guns" that deliver extra-tight patterns at longer and longer ranges. Special extra-tight, screw-in turkey chokes are available that can tighten the pattern of any shotgun and make it shoot deadly patterns considerably farther than it did before.

I'm all for tight chokes, but the long-range situations for which these guns are touted need some examination.

My uneasiness with so-called long-range turkey guns occurs because as the effective range of his shotgun increases, it becomes natural for a hunter to take longer and longer shots. As a result a lot of turkeys are crippled and lost at long range—birds that could have been killed outright if the hunter had waited until they came into absolute killing range.

The current emphasis on long-range turkey guns ignores the primary challenge of turkey hunting, which is to bring the turkey in very close to you. It replaces that challenge with the suggestion that

Specialty "turkey" guns are now offered that deliver extra-heavy, very tight shot patterns at longer range. These guns are very effective within their limits, but they may encourage you to take long shots rather than wait for a shot that is within absolute killing range.

it's okay to make use of a technical advantage to shoot turkeys at ranges that require less hunting skill.

There is always a limit to how far any gun will deliver a lethal pattern, regardless of how it is choked. At some point its pattern becomes too open to guarantee a kill.

The real thrill of turkey hunting for most of us is not killing a bird at excessive range but seeing a wild turkey approach. There is nothing quite like the sensation of watching a wary gobbler come closer and closer, knowing that his eye is alert for any danger and that the slightest movement will spook him.

This is a bird whose exceptional eyesight and instinctive wariness sometimes make him seem an impossible quarry. Yet when you do everything right—call convincingly and don't move—you *can* watch that bird come closer and closer until he's within such a short distance that any full-choked 12-gauge shotgun will put a lethal dose of shot in his head and neck and kill him outright. This is what turkey hunting is all about.

Rather than chasing the dubious pot of gold of longer-ranged shotguns, I suggest that you'll become a better hunter and succeed more often if you concentrate on sitting still, learn to call convincingly, and use turkey decoys to help make gobblers take those extra steps that bring them within the killing range of any full-choked 12-gauge shotgun.

It's often not difficult to get a gobbler to approach to within 50 or 60 yards. But at that range the turkey often hangs up and refuses to come closer. He'll strut and gobble and spit and drum and put on a big show, but now he wants the hen he's been hearing to show herself and go to him.

You only have a few moments at this critical stage, for if the gobbler fails to see the hen he's been hearing his natural wariness will warn him that something is wrong, and he'll drift away.

Knowing that he isn't likely to stay long, a turkey hunter hooked on the long-range gun idea is likely to decide to shoot at this juncture. "He's not going to come any closer," he thinks. "I'm gonna try him."

So he takes careful aim and shoots. Now, it's not hard to hit a turkey at 50 or 60 yards. So the hunter will hit the bird—but will he kill it? Probably not, because only pellets that strike the bony area of a gobbler's head or neck are lethal at this range. Now consider what would have happened if the hunter had been using decoys and had not been convinced that his gun was capable of long-range kills.

The gobbler would have come to within 50 or 60 yards of where he had been hearing a hen calling, and would have hung up just the same. But as he went through his strutting display he would have seen the decoys and been reassured that what he had been hearing was, indeed, a hen turkey.

Decoys make excellent range markers. If your decoys are set at 20 yards you know that a gobbler is within absolute killing range when he gets close to them.

Special extra-tight, screw-in turkey chokes like this Gobblin' Thunder model from Kick's Industries will give you patterns that destroy a pie plate at up to 40 yards.

So this time, rather than refusing to come closer or drifting away, the gobbler would have probably come on in, a few steps at a time, continuing to strut, gobble, spit, and drum, and giving the hunter a wonderful show to remember. When he finally reaches the decoys the gobbler will be about 20 yards away. At that range, with any full-choked 12-gauge shotgun you will either kill the bird or miss him entirely.

That being said, I must admit that I have added a Gobblin' Thunder extra-tight turkey choke from Kick's Industries (698 Magnolia Church Road, Statesboro, GA 30458, 1-800-587-2779) to the 12-gauge pump I most often use for turkey hunting. Even though I really want to wait for the close shot and use decoys to help bring the bird all the way in, there have been times when I've been unable to get the bird to come as close as I wanted and have taken slightly longer shots.

When that happens I want to be shooting a pattern so dense there will be no question about its lethality.

CUSTOMIZING YOUR TURKEY GUN

A turkey gun should not be shiny. Turkeys notice everything that seems unnatural and, while they may sometimes approach a shiny object without alarm, if that shiny object moves they are going to focus on it.

Today's specialty turkey guns come with baked-on camouflage finishes that do much to make them less noticeable in the turkey woods. Camouflage adhesive tape, sold in most stores that sell bow-hunting or turkey-hunting supplies, can be applied over the shiny finish of any gun to make it blend harmoniously with the forest floor. Since the tape can be removed, the gun is not permanently altered.

Another, less common technique for camouflaging turkey guns is to remove the bluing by applying commercial bluing and rust remover; you then brown the metal rather than rebluing it. Commercial browning compound and the bluing and rust remover are available at most gun stores. (I have used Birchwood-Casey products successfully.)

Browned barrels have a very natural, earthy look that is not shiny and appeals to my sense of naturalness. You can remove the shiny varnished finish on the stock using

Removing the shiny bluing from a turkey gun's barrel and replacing it with a dull brown finish made this double-barreled 12-gauge much less noticeable when a gobbler drew near.

wood alcohol and steel wool. (If a stock has a plastic finish, this can be scraped off with a piece of broken glass.) Once the shiny finish is removed a dull, natural finish can be achieved by wetting the stock with linseed oil and wiping it dry, but not polishing it.

A shotgun with a dull, natural wood stock and dull, brown barrel looks like any other piece of forest litter in the turkey woods.

SHOT SIZE

Turkeys have been killed with literally every pellet size, but those who commonly shoot turkeys at close range use #5 and #6 shot more than any other. These pellet sizes are heavy enough to penetrate deeply at short range; there are also enough pellets in commercial magnum turkey loads to make a very dense pattern.

Most of the expert turkey hunters I know use either #5 or #6 pellets to produce a dense pattern for their first shot, which will be at the turkey's head, and back that up with bone-breaking #4s or #2s in case they have to shoot at the bony back of a bird that is running or flying away after the first shot failed.

You can only determine the shot size that is right for your gun by shooting various loads and seeing which one patterns best in your gun. A good pattern for turkey hunting consistently puts more than 20 pellets in a drawing of a gobbler's head and neck at whatever range you decide will be your maximum. If you use decoys and set them at a bit under 20 yards from your shooting position, most of your shots will be at ranges of 25 yards or less.

Nickel-plated and copper-plated shot is available from major ammunition makers. These more expensive loads are worth the added expense because their hard plating reduces deformation of the pellets that come into contact with the barrel when the load squeezes through the choke; consequently, more pellets fly true. My favorite turkey gun places at least 10 percent more shot in a turkey-head target when I use plated shot.

Magnum loads? Always use them. There will be plenty of times when any shotgun shell would prove lethal, but maximum pattern density is achieved by putting all the pellets out there that you can. The time will come when maximum pattern density makes a dead bird out of one that would have been wounded by a less dense pattern.

A 2-ounce load of shot in a 12-gauge, 3-inch magnum shell contains 33 percent more pellets than the 1½-ounce load contained in a typical 12-gauge, 2¾-inch shell. Even more impressive, a 2¼-ounce load in a 3-inch magnum shell contains 50 percent more pellets than the 2¾-inch, 1½-ounce load.

When your target is as small as a turkey's head and neck, maximum-density loads that put more shot in the target area really pay off. Although it is true that the lighter loads have greater velocity, the magnum loads still deliver the pellets on target at velocities that result in lethal penetration beyond the distance at which patterns fail.

20

MUZZLELOADERS FOR TURKEYS

Except for all the fire and smoke, I assumed that hunting turkeys with a muzzleloading shotgun wouldn't be much different from using a modern gun. I started finding out how wrong I was as soon as I slid my new muzzleloader from the box and headed out behind the barn to pattern it.

For tradition's sake I had ordered from Dixie Gun Works a 12-gauge, double-barreled caplock gun made in Italy by David Pedersoli for Navy Arms. The recommended load was 95 grains of FFg or Pyrodex and an equal volume of shot. No specific wad combination was mentioned. That was up to me to figure out.

GETTING ACQUAINTED

I drew a turkey head on a piece of typewriter paper, pinned it

Muzzleloading black-powder shotguns like this 12-gauge Pedersoli can make excellent turkey guns, but you need to experiment to find the shot, powder, and wad combination that shoots the tightest patterns in each individual gun.

to a log, backed off 30 steps, loaded up, and took careful aim. When the thing went off it nearly knocked me off my feet. I haven't been kicked that hard since I was a small boy and made the mistake of holding my uncle's duck gun away from my shoulder in a misguided attempt to avoid recoil.

Gritting my teeth, I took aim with the second barrel, fired, and flinched so badly that I missed the target altogether.

I got out a big box for a target in order to see where the shot was going, and after two more bruising explosions determined that the gun was shooting wide to the left. It was throwing worthless doughnut patterns with 20-inch holes in the centers. And by now the recoil had me flinching so badly that I had to rest the forend on a stump to hold my point of aim.

So far my experience had confirmed the most important fact about shooting a muzzleloading shotgun: You don't just take one out of the box and go hunting. First you have to learn a lot about the gun.

MAKING IT FIT

Although I had looked forward to carrying this light 6½-pounder, the gun needed to be heavier in order to handle stout turkey loads without delivering punishing recoil.

"I can pour a pound of melted lead into a piece of copper tubing and fit that into a hole bored in the butt of the stock," our local gunsmith Ben Kilham advised. "That will reduce the recoil considerably. It won't hurt the balance of the gun because this gun (like many muzzleloaders) is muzzle heavy anyway."

Then Ben had me mount the gun. He studied the fit, then said, "Either your face is too fat or the stock is too thick." He suggested bending the stock to make the gun fit so that it would deliver its pattern exactly where I pointed it.

Next Ben noted another important consideration. "In turkey hunting you'll be shooting at a stationary target, not a rising bird, so you'll need to keep your head down. If you shoot with your head up, you'll shoot high."

To keep my eye in line with the barrel he added a rear bead on the rib a few inches ahead of the hammers. "Now you just have to line up the sights like you do with a rifle," he said.

Finally he measured the chokes in each barrel. "Nothing wrong there," he reported. "They're both very tight. Your doughnut patterns must be caused by the wads blowing through the shot string. You're going to have to experiment with your loads."

ANOTHER SHOT

The next day I was out behind the barn again.

This time I loaded with a light charge to reduce recoil and overcome my expectation that this gun was going to hurt. I shot it half a dozen times with light loads, then snapped a cap on an empty barrel to see if I was still flinching. I was pleased to find that the gun's muzzle no longer moved when I squeezed the trigger.

Flinching ruins accuracy when you're shooting any gun, but with a muzzleloader the effect is even worse because of the time it takes the hammer to fall after you release the trigger. If you flinch this relatively slow lock time permits your point of aim to change dramatically before the charge leaves the barrel. So you must concentrate on holding your aim through the shot—just as ballplayers concentrate on hitting through the ball.

When turkey hunting, you need the tightest pattern a gun can throw. Your target is the tiny, bony structure of a gobbler's head and neck—something about the size of a lemon with a large stringbean attached.

GETTING ON TARGET

Initially I tried using modern plastic shot cups in place of traditional fiber wads, thinking the cups would create the tightest patterns, but there were problems. Although I tried a variety of products I couldn't find a shot cup that could be loaded through the gun's extra-tight chokes without being damaged in the process. In addition, the patterns were inconsistent. Sometimes the shot never left the cup; instead the cup would tumble in flight and fly backward, still loaded with shot, to blow through the target like a slug. Other times the shot left the cup but the pattern was scattered.

Eventually I gave up on plastic shot cups and began experimenting with traditional wadding. I had a package of thick 12-gauge fiber wads, but I found it impossible to push them through the tight chokes. Smaller 13-gauge fiber wads will fit through the chokes in a tightly choked 12-gauge gun, but they don't make a tight-enough seal between the powder and shot, and they cause badly blown patterns.

Finally I found the answer in a package of Thompson/Center Natural Wads—lubricated woven-wool wads only ⅛-inch thick. The thin construction of these wads allows the material to compress as it is pushed through the chokes; it then expands to its original diameter and fills the larger part of the bore, creating a tight seal. Two Natural Wads pushed down on top of the powder are easy to load and expand to seal the barrel adequately.

On top of the shot charge I used two thin cardboard wads that are flexible enough to be pressed through the chokes singly without difficulty and, when paired, tight enough to hold the shot in place, even when I carry the gun around for long periods of time with the muzzle pointed toward the ground.

Shooting 90 grains of Pyrodex and an equal volume of #6 soft lead shot with this wad combination gave me patterns that were respectable, but there was room for improvement. I still wanted more shot in the center of the pattern.

I figured that switching to nickel-plated hard lead shot would reduce the number of pellets that escaped the pattern because they were deformed as they compressed upon passing through the choke.

I made this change and immediately saw improved density in the center of the pattern.

Since I would be shooting at a stationary target rather than a fast-moving flying bird, the velocity of my shot string was less important than the number of pellets I delivered on target. So without altering the 90-grain powder charge I increased my shot load to a volume equaling 100 grains (a bit more than 1¼ ounces of the nickel-plated shot). I always use decoys to bring the turkeys into very close range, so I also shortened my shooting range to 25 yards.

When the smoke cleared from that next shot I counted 43 holes in the sketch of the turkey's head. My second shot put 37 holes in the vital area.

Finally, I had found my load.

My time-consuming experience is not unusual. Muzzle-loading shotguns have idiosyncrasies that make them more challenging than modern shotguns to shoot well, but there is considerable satisfaction to be gained from learning how to make a gun shoot the way you want it to.

I was now confident that I could make this gun deliver a dense pattern of shot within a small target at acceptable range. I'd managed it on a paper target, and now I felt ready to go turkey hunting.

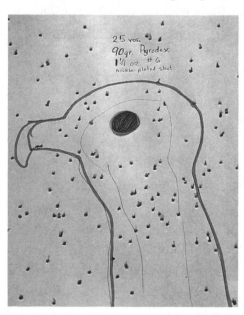

When my muzzleloader began throwing shot patterns with density like this at 25 yards I knew I had found the right load for my gun.

THE FINAL TEST

I am pleased to report that when the climactic moment arrived, the muzzleloading shotgun rose to my shoulder smoothly and shot

true. But after all my efforts to make this gun deliver a tight pattern at moderate range, the first turkey I killed with it was only 6 yards away when I fired.

The gobbler had circled me and approached from the wrong side. I couldn't turn without spooking him. When he finally stepped into my shooting zone he was so close that there was no room for the pattern to open up. It was almost like shoot-

I loaded nickel-plated lead shot to get the tightest shot pattern I could from my muzzleloader the day I shot this big Eastern gobbler in New Hampshire.

ing him with a rifle. Luckily the stock fitted me

well, and the rear bead we had added reminded me to get my face down tight on the stock; when the gun came up I was right on target.

ANOTHER MUZZLELOADER TURKEY HUNT

I had a better chance to prove the value of determining the right load for this gun on a hunt in the Georgia mountains a year later.

Two longbeards had come together to my calls and had just discovered the decoys. At first they marched in shoulder to shoulder, but as they drew closer to the decoys one bird decided that he did not want a confrontation. He stopped and let his companion go in alone.

Thinking that the shy bird would soon gain confidence and rejoin his more aggressive brother (and greedily hoping to make a double kill), I held off as the aggressive bird came into range. He went all the way to the jake decoy and checked it out, discovering the ruse.

As he began to shy away I clucked to him, hoping to anchor him in place. Instead my call, coming from a spot where he could see there was no turkey, only increased his sense that something was wrong. Now he stepped away with a worried air.

By the time I realized that I could not stop him and turn him back by calling, he was 35 yards away and leaving.

I raised the muzzleloader, aimed at his extended neck, and concentrated on holding through the shot. The hammer fell, the gun boomed, and the scene disappeared in a cloud of smoke.

But when it cleared the old longbeard was flopping dead on the ground 37 steps from my shooting position. I checked his head and neck and counted 17 pellet wounds in the vital target area.

That's as tight as any turkey gun needs to shoot.

21

A HORSEBACK
HUNT IN THE
BLACK HILLS

In the woods at dawn the sound of a turkey gobbling at close range
can be positively levitating. It can lift you 6 inches off the ground
and hold you there.

This one let go about two trees away from where I sat just
under the crest of a ridge on the eastern edge of the Black Hills in
South Dakota. John Hauer and I had roosted the bird the evening
before. We had ridden out on horseback from John's Turkey Track
Ranch and stopped to call from vantage points that looked down
over flowered alpine meadows and timbered ridges to the prairie
far beyond.

Late in the afternoon we got an answer from the other side of a
limestone canyon. We worked that bird until sunset, calling and getting gobbles in return, but the turkey wouldn't come our way.

At John Hauer's Turkey Track Ranch in Piedmont, South Dakota, hunters ride smooth-gaited Paso horses to reach turkey-hunting grounds in the Black Hills. Once a gobbler is located the horses are hidden and tied, and the hunt proceeds on foot.

"He must have a bunch of hens with him," John said. "He's afraid if he leaves, some other old gobbler will steal them away."

So we followed, staying about 300 yards from where the turkey's gobbles told us he was. John called repeatedly, using an old cedar box and a mouthful of diaphragm calls to plead with the gobbler in the most seductive tones. But the old boy was clearly a chauvinist. "You want something from me, you had better come over here," his gobbles demanded.

We followed along for about a mile, but when sunset came we were still just about as far behind.

"We'll wait here," John said. "Once he's on his roost we'll get a good bearing on where he is and come back in the morning."

A few minutes later I began a series of intermittent coyote howls, to which the gobbler responded with defiant declarations, while John crept in closer to get a better idea of where the turkey had roosted.

Under starlight we rode the horses back to the ranch while owls hooted on the ridges and coyotes yipped and sang in chorus from the prairie edge.

"I know about where he is," John said. "We'll ride in there early and get within about 100 yards of his roosting tree an hour before daylight. We'll cluck a couple of times before he's off the roost to let him know there's a lonely hen close by, and when he flies down a few yelps ought to bring him in."

It seemed like a perfect setup, but that night I lay awake reviewing all the things that had gone wrong on other turkey hunts when the end had seemed equally predictable.

I remembered the times they'd sneaked behind me and come in from the one direction I couldn't point my gun; when they'd sailed out of roosting trees and flown downhill to some other turkey's or turkey hunter's plaintive yelps; and when they'd flown down and just plain disappeared.

An hour before dawn John and I crept over the crest of the ridge and settled in against a pair of big ponderosa pine trunks close to where we figured the gobbler had roosted.

I scrootched down to burrow out a comfortable seat and dug my heels into the sandy soil to provide foot support. Then I laid my gun across my knees with the butt up under my shoulder; this way I'd only have to lift the muzzle a few inches and swing the gun slightly to cover a wide-open area 25 yards in front of me.

I pulled my camouflage bandanna up over my nose and mouth, leaned my head back against the tree, and closed my eyes for a moment. When I opened them, I saw the turkey.

Against the morning starlight I could plainly make out a barrel-shaped object just two trees in front of me. A few moments later it moved. Now I could see the tail feathers lift and fall when the turkey shifted his weight from one foot to the other.

By some fluke we had come in too close. Instead of creeping into the 100-yard range we had hoped for, John and I had settled down almost under the roosting tree.

When the first light of dawn began to brighten the sky John eased off a couple of sleepy clucks and a kind of yawning yelp that woke the gobbler instantly. He swelled up in his tree and burst forth with a gobble that lifted me off the ground; while I was still in the air he double-gobbled, and every hair on my body prickled.

Now he jumped from limb to limb until he was on our side of the roosting tree. Then he gobbled again. For the next hour the gobbler studied us from his tree limb. He was only 20 yards from where I sat—so close that when he threw his head forward and opened his beak to gobble I could see his tongue. In that hour, as the dimness of dawn turned to daylight, the turkey must have gobbled 50 times. Each time he let go I flinched.

I couldn't move. A mosquito walked around on the bridge of my nose for a while and then started drilling on my eyelid. I had a cramp in my right leg. Ponderosa pollen always makes me sneeze, but I didn't. I just concentrated on stillness.

John was frozen beneath his tree, too. The turkey was studying us, looking for the hen he had heard right where John was sitting. All we could do was wait and hope that he would drop down in front of us.

I picked the place I thought the turkey would land. "Raise the gun while he's still in the air and looking at his landing place, and get the bead on his head the instant he hits the ground," I told myself. I'd have to shoot before he puffed up and went into strut because a gobbler pulls his head and neck down into the protective concavity in his breast then.

"Shoot when he's standing with his head and neck up," John tells his hunters. "Don't shoot when he sticks his neck out to gobble, 'cause when he's through he'll pull his head in quick and you'll shoot where it was but isn't."

And then, after one more gobble, the turkey flew down amid a thrashing of wings and breaking twigs and branches. But instead of landing where I expected the gobbler flew to my right and set down only 12 paces away, just over my right shoulder in that awful spot where you can't swing a gun when you need to.

I couldn't swing with him. I just spun on my rump, saw the bead come even with the blazing red head, and squeezed before either the turkey or I could assess the situation.

As I jumped up to run to the dead gobbler John stopped me.

"Wait a minute," he said. "There's a tradition I like to follow when a hunter gets a turkey. We've had a good hunt. You've seen some grand country and you've killed a turkey and now your hunt is over. I'm going to leave you alone now with your turkey. Take a few minutes to consider what it's all been about."

So while John went to get the horses, I sat there with a dead turkey and watched a new day wash across the prairie and blossom on the timbered ridges. It was a beautiful scene, one that the turkey had been part of every day of his life until I crept in and removed him from it. This could only be justified if the turkey would be appreciated and put to good use. I vowed to make sure that he was served on the table with respect and gratitude. On a distant ridge another gobbler sounded off, ready to take my turkey's place in nature's scheme.

John Hauer of Piedmont, South Dakota, could be considered the dean of Black Hills turkey hunters. He is certainly one of the most enthusiastic and knowledgeable, and his Turkey Track Ranch outfitting business accounts for success rates that were once unheard of in turkey-hunting circles. Year in, year out, 85 percent of those who hunt from Turkey Track Ranch get their bird.

"We've got a lot of turkeys, a lot of country to hunt, and guides who can really talk turkey," John admits.

The Hauers' son, Bo, has been one of the top turkey callers in the Black Hills since he was a schoolboy. He's been guiding turkey hunters since he was 11 and has racked up an impressive list of successes.

"Hunters used to object when we showed them Bo and said he'd be their guide," John recalls. "He always had to be back in time to meet the school bus. But you know, most of the time he'd get them a turkey with time to spare."

Horseback riding adds a dimension to turkey hunting that few hunters have considered or had the opportunity to experience. Among other things, horses let you get into country that is far beyond the early-morning reach of hunters traveling on foot. Riding is comfortable, too, especially when you use the Peruvian Paso horses that John and his wife, Nancy, raise.

Pasos are known as the smoothest-gaited horses there are. "Just like riding a bike," John says.

I rode with the Hauers for three days and can attest to the

smooth gait these horses have. They shuffle along at a fast pace with no bounce, eating up the miles without abusing even the sorriest of riders.

As we rode through the forest on a quiet floor of sand and pine needles, John would rein up every so often and make a series of calls. If he got an answer we would ride as close as he thought was safe, tie the horses, and work toward the turkeys on foot until we were close enough to settle in and try to get a gobbler to approach.

Not wanting to end my hunt too soon, I passed up a jake that came in with half a dozen hens the first afternoon. Later a bigger gobbler walked in with another bunch of hens but never presented a proper shot.

The cream-colored tips of this gobbler's tail feathers identify it as a Merriam—a strain of wild turkeys that has been successfully established throughout mountainous regions in the West.

The Merriam strain of wild turkey is native to the southwestern states and is associated with ponderosa pine and country where the annual rainfall is less than 25 inches. Pine seeds make up a large part of the Merriam's diet, as do grasshoppers and other insects whose moisture content compensates for the limited water sources.

The Black Hills have a natural timber mix of ponderosa pine and burr oak that provides a heavy crop of nutritious seeds and acorns. Big brown-and-yellow grasshoppers thrive in the alpine meadows. The entire Black Hills region, in fact, is an ideal haven for turkeys, but it is an island of suitable habitat surrounded by miles of open prairie on which turkeys could not exist.

"They just never got here," John Hauer explains. "But when they were introduced by man, they sure caught on."

Like all wild turkeys, Black Hills gobblers react to calling in a variety of ways. Toward the end of the mating season, when most of the hens have mated and stolen away to begin sitting on their eggs, the gobblers are really on the prowl, looking for leftover hens. That's when they're most likely to come to a call.

When they're at the peak of the mating season the dominant gobblers are usually traveling with a bevy of hens, which they're afraid they'll lose to another gobbler if they sneak off to check out the sounds of a seductively yelping distant hen. At this point they will answer your calls and gobble and gobble, but they won't leave their hens. You have to sneak in close to this kind of gobbler and hope you can convince him to leave his harem just long enough for an illicit quickie.

Only the dominant males in a given group mate with hens. The dominant bird may have a few nonbreeding males traveling with him, and they will gobble and strut, but they'll be driven away by the dominant bird whenever they show interest in a hen. Often these birds are afraid to go to the sounds of a yelping hen for fear of another drubbing from the head turkey. These nonbreeders can drive you crazy. They'll answer every call but make no attempt to come in, and when you try to sneak up on one and call from close in, the bird may very well run.

"A gobbler's trophy value shouldn't be measured only by the length of his beard or spurs, or his weight," John Hauer insists. "Any spring gobbler is a trophy, and I'd prefer to rate them by how exciting and how challenging they make the hunt. To my way of thinking, a 20-pounder with a 10-inch beard that comes right in isn't as much of a trophy as a smaller bird that makes you sweet-talk him for an hour or more before he'll come to you."

The Black Hills spring gobbler season traditionally begins the first weekend in April and continues through the first weekend in May. It is a promising time of year, fresh and green; in the stillness of dawn, before the wind comes up, you can hear for miles.

At this time of day, with gobblers sounding off on the ridges, it seems as if there must be turkeys everywhere. One turkey's gobble triggers the next one up the line and soon the mountainsides ring with the challenging mating calls of the wariest birds in the woods. It's an exhilarating experience just being there.

Canoes and small boats give you access to turkey habitat that may be too far from roads to attract other hunters. Sometimes all you have to do is cross a narrow piece of water to reach country where turkeys have never been disturbed.

22

CANOE CAMPING FOR TURKEYS

On a sweltering May afternoon five weeks after turkey season opened on the Cheyenne River Sioux Indian Reservation in South Dakota, I climbed to the top of a prairie bluff and sat down. This is where the Sioux man had told me to go. He said it was an ancient watching place from which Sioux braves had scouted the movements of buffalo and deer and U.S. cavalry in the old days.

"It's a good place for watching and listening," he said.

From this vantage point I surveyed five wide river bends and an expanse of undulating prairie and forested river bottom that reached from the eastern to the western horizon. Far out on the prairie I could see several Indian ranch houses a mile or two apart. The gravel road that connected them disappeared over a ridge three miles to the north. When a pickup truck came over that ridge I could see the plume of dust it raised for a long time before I could hear the tires crunching gravel.

There was no wind and sounds seemed amplified in the hot still air. When three horses came out of the timber in the river bottom and began grazing in a meadow a quarter mile below me, I could hear them chewing. When a pair of wood ducks flitted out through the cottonwoods and splashed down several hundred yards downriver, the loudness of the sound startled me.

Afternoon passed into evening, and the sounds increased as the shadows lengthened. Pheasants crowed. I heard a click and turned to spot two deer moving on a trail through the brush on the next ridge. A dog barked far away. Cattle lowed and stamped their feet; the thuds were like drumbeats. Birds in brilliant mating plumage shifted about with whirring wings and raucous proclamations of territorial prerogative.

At 7:50 I heard the turkey. He was about half a mile east in the center of a big patch of timber across the river from the places hunters on foot would be likely to go. Between 8 and 8:30 the turkey gobbled 12 more times, and when I left the listening place at dark I had a good fix on where he was roosted.

"Just what we expected," John Cooper nodded when I returned to our riverbank tent camp and told him what I'd heard. John had not roosted a turkey himself but had seen a bunch earlier in the day and had a good idea where he could find them the next morning.

"They were across the river, just like yours," he said. "That's where they go when they sense danger."

Like deer, wild turkeys everywhere are quick to react to hunting pressure. When they sense that they are being hunted the birds withdraw to the sections of their range that hunters find most difficult to reach. Depending on the type of terrain, they may head for the ridges or slink far back into the swamps. If there's a river handy you can bet that turkeys will cross to the side where human access is more limited.

This retreat of turkeys to the far side of the river was exactly what we were counting on. We had made camp on a riverbank deep within good turkey country and planned to use a canoe to reach the sections of river-bottom forest that were most difficult to reach by vehicle or on foot.

"Nobody out here uses a canoe to hunt turkeys," John confided. "Even though the season has been open for more than a month and the hunting pressure has been heavy, we'll have these birds all to ourselves."

The next morning we crossed the river before dawn and hiked upstream to a natural opening among the cottonwoods 150 yards from where I had put the gobbler to bed.

We chose a place that backed up against dense brush with an overstory of large roosting trees. It was close to thick cover and across the river from places turkeys associated with human activity, so we felt that a gobbler would not be afraid to come to our location.

From his pack John took out three folding foam turkey decoys: two hens and a jake. He placed the hens a few feet apart in the open and the jake about 20 yards off to the side. I sat in a dark hollow at the base of an old cottonwood facing parallel to the riverbank. John sat against another tree 30 yards away facing toward the thick woods.

As the dawn sky brightened we heard the gobbler greet the new day with a booming challenge from his tree branch deep inside the woods.

John answered a moment later with a creaky lonesome-hen call. His chalked cedar box call made her sound sleepy, still on her roost. When the gobbler answered with an excited double gobble John did not return the call. It was still a bit too early. He didn't want the turkey to come just yet.

Suddenly my eye was caught by a dark shape on a tree branch that overhung the river a little more than 100 yards downstream. As daylight increased I could see that it was a hen turkey, one of the gobbler's harem.

"If she flies down before the gobbler starts coming to us, we're screwed," I thought. "He'll go to her instead."

In the woods the gobbler sounded off again. His voice was a bit muffled now; it sounded like he was off his roost and on the ground.

There was no way to signal John about the hen in the tree, but I did my best to will the hen to stay put while the other side of my brain willed John to start calling. Apparently the telepathy worked.

The hen shifted on her limb but did not fly down, and a moment later John began the most seductive series of yelps I've ever heard come out of a cedar box call. He put everything but the flutter of eyelids into that call; somehow he stroked a lubricous little whimper into the end of each plaintive yelp, too. It was a call guaranteed to make any gobbler throw out his chest, fan his tail, drag his wings, and flash his head red, white, and blue.

When the turkey gobbled a moment later he was halfway to us.

I glanced over at John in time to see him slip the box call into his pocket and pop a diaphragm call into his mouth. Then he began a run of yelps that ended with an excited cackle.

This was too much for the gobbler. He didn't even bother to answer. A moment later I caught movement straight out in front, and then I could see the whole of him, coming at a fast trot, right at me.

The gobbler burst into our clearing 40 or 50 yards away, then slammed on the brakes and went into full strut. When he went sleek and gobbled, John responded with three soft clucks that turned the gobbler's head in his direction.

When he saw the decoys the gobbler puffed up to the size of a small bear, strutted, spat out a declarative drum note, and rattled his wings. Then he began to stalk the decoys. The jake decoy was off to the right, and the gobbler's clear intent was to drive that jake off at once.

Every step brought him closer on a route that would pass within 20 yards of where I sat on the ground, my Browning pump laid across my legs.

The only cover between us was one large cottonwood tree. As the gobbler walked behind the trunk I slipped off the safety and shouldered my gun, and when he came into view on the other side of the tree I put the bead just below his blatantly crimson head and fired.

The range was 20 yards, the choke was extra full, and the Federal load of 2 ounces of copper-plated #6 shot caught him entirely in the head and neck. It put his lights out instantly.

"Perfect!" John crowed. "That's the way it's supposed to work."

The canoe had given us the ability to hunt an area other hunters found too difficult to reach. By camping close by we'd been able to get back to the remote roosting tree and set up before dawn.

"The canoe lets you go where the turkeys go when they get pushed around by hunters," John said.

An hour after I killed my gobbler, John located the bunch he had seen the

John Cooper used a canoe to cross the little river that separated this big Merriam's home territory from land that was easily accessible from the road. Where turkeys are not pressured by other hunters they are more likely to respond to calling.

day before. Again, they were on the less accessible side of the river in a patch of brushy woods. A loud exploratory run of yelps from John's cedar box had brought a booming gobble from the head turkey.

Quickly John moved to a natural opening, put out the decoys, and sat down to talk turkey. The gobbler answered three times from the same spot then went silent. The next time he stopped to gobble he was close, and John switched to his mouth call once more.

I was sitting behind John without a gun, hoping for a picture opportunity as the turkey came in, but this fellow didn't take time to stop and pose. When I saw his red head bobbing toward us he was coming at a fast walk; he never stopped until he entered the clearing at a range of 25 yards and John fired.

"That's why I always use decoys," John said. "The decoys bring the gobbler those extra few yards closer that put him in absolute killing range and let you make a clean head shot. You never cripple a bird. Either you kill him or you miss.

"Decoys help to stop the turkey so that you can get a good aim at his head," he continued. "Gobblers always stop and strut when they see the decoys. Then they stalk them, stopping every few steps to strut again. You can take time to aim and shoot when you're ready."

John has used decoys religiously ever since he missed a big gobbler one time when he had failed to put his decoys out.

"I had the decoys with me but for some reason I just didn't bother putting them out," he recalled. "The gobbler came to my call and never stopped. When he didn't see a turkey at the place where the calls had been coming from, he ran in and went right past me. I guess he thought the calling hen had moved out in back of me. He got so far around to my right that I was all bound up and missed when I shot, even though the turkey was very close.

"If the decoys had been out he would have stopped," John lamented. "I've used them ever since that day."

Historically, most of South Dakota was not natural wild turkey range. Turkeys have become established throughout the forested river bottoms and in the pine forests of the Black Hills over the past 30 years, however, as a result of very successful trap and transplant programs conducted by state and tribal wildlife agencies.

From an initial stocking of 8 Merriam wild turkeys, in exchange for which South Dakota gave New Mexico 25 sage hens in 1948, and 15 Merriams, for which the state gave Colorado 2,500 channel catfish in 1950, the statewide wild turkey population has grown to about 40,000 birds.

The first birds were released in the vast canyoned forests of the Black Hills. As the turkey population increased there birds were trapped and transplanted to more locations. By 1953 turkeys were well established in the Black Hills region, and the state began transplanting them to the forested river bottoms that bisect the open prairie.

According to the journals of Lewis and Clark, in 1804 wild turkeys did not exist along the Missouri River north of a place about where Yankton, South Dakota, now stands in the southeastern corner of the state. In the past 30 years, however, turkeys have established themselves and spread so successfully that the state now offers spring and autumn seasons in 14 counties west of the Missouri River and 3 East River counties.

In the 1970s the Cheyenne River Sioux tribe began releasing turkeys in the Cheyenne and Moreau River bottoms; today the wild turkey population on this 1.3-million-acre tract of tribal land has risen to more than 4,000 birds. In recent years the Cheyenne River Sioux have been trapping and transplanting turkeys to other Sioux reservations in the state. Fast-growing populations now exist on the

Standing Rock, Lower Brule, and Sisseton-Wahpeton Sioux reservations as well.

Hunting success rates on the South Dakota prairie during the spring gobbler season have been averaging better then 60 percent in recent years. In 1988 state-licensed South Dakota prairie turkey hunters scored an exceptionally high 74 percent success rate. Hunter success has been even higher on the Cheyenne River Sioux Indian Reservation since 1989, when the tribe first opened its lands to nontribal hunters.

The high success rates are due to concentrated turkey populations and relatively low numbers of turkey hunters. On the prairie, turkeys are concentrated in the narrow bands of forest that border rivers and in brushy draws. They feed along the edge of the open prairie but are rarely found far from trees. This narrows the areas that hunters must survey to find turkeys; the silence of the prairie makes it easier to locate a roosting gobbler at evening and to stay within calling range of moving turkeys during daylight hours.

On tribal lands the forested river bottoms, brushy draws, and much of the prairie itself remain relatively unchanged from how they always were. Cattle graze the land instead of buffalo, and there are stock fences, but the habitat is natural and game is plentiful.

For specific Indian reservation season and license information, contact: Cheyenne River Sioux Tribe Game, Fish and Parks Department, P.O. Box 590, Eagle Butte, SD 57625 (605-964-7812).

For information regarding turkey hunting on public and private lands in South Dakota, write: Game, Fish and Parks Department, 445 East Capitol, Pierre, SD 57501-3185 (605-773-3485).

23

HOW TO HUNT GOBBLERS IN THE FALL

Fall gobbler hunting has won a well-deserved reputation as the ultimate exercise in frustration. Mature male turkeys rarely respond to calling in the fall and are often almost impossible to influence in any way. This is why most turkey hunters forget about mature gobblers in the fall and use the autumn turkey season to concentrate on young, tender poults—which eagerly respond to calling.

"Gobblers just don't give a damn about other turkeys in the fall," says Tad Brown. "They do group up in the autumn, but if they get separated they're not frantic to get back together. You can call forever with the best-sounding calls a man can make and a fall gobbler may not even care enough to answer, much less come to you. You might as well just leave your calls at home."

That's an unexpected statement coming from a man who is one of Missouri's most consistently successful spring gobbler callers, a high-ranking competition caller, and a well-known turkey-call designer.

Yet despite his belief that calling fall gobblers is a waste of time Tad Brown kills a mature gobbler or two almost every autumn, proving that fall gobbler hunting can be successful. Last October I met him on his home ground at Truman Lake near Warsaw, Missouri, to see how he does it.

"I stalk 'em," he explained. "Just like hunting deer. I locate a gobbler flock and sneak in on them."

Now, Tad is a big man. If animals hunted people he would be a trophy. And in October the Missouri turkey woods are ankle deep in dry oak and hickory leaves that don't just rustle, they clatter. I found it hard to believe that a man of Tad's stature could move through those noisy woods quietly enough to get within absolute killing range of a group of the wariest, sharpest-eyed, keenest-eared birds in the forest.

"I just move real slow," he told me. "You can't just step on your foot, you have to press it down slowly, crushing the leaves with a soft

and even sound. Then wait and get balanced before you advance the next foot."

To locate a flock of gobblers in the fall Tad heads for big water. His favorite hunting ground is the narrow strip of open land between the forest and the water's edge that extends for hundreds of miles along the jagged shores of the 55,000-acre Truman Lake, and his method of hunting works wherever turkey habitat borders on a public waterway.

"The open strip of weedy floodplain between the forest and the shoreline of any lake, reservoir, or river is a natural gathering place for turkeys in the autumn," Tad explains. "If the weather is dry they come to drink at the water's edge, and if it's raining they come out into open places to get away from the heavy droplets that fall from trees in the woods. Regardless of the weather, turkeys spend a lot of time in shoreline areas feeding on weed seeds and grasshoppers.

"You could ride roads looking for gobbler flocks loafing in open places, but if you locate one you then have to find the property owner and ask permission to hunt. By the time you've got permission the turkeys will have moved," Tad notes.

The beauty of hunting an Army Corps of Engineers reservoir like Truman Lake is that the shoreline is all publicly owned, and most of it is open to hunting. You can cruise along in a boat checking the shoreline until you spot a flock of turkeys and then figure out how best to stalk them.

Tad has been guiding, hunting, fishing, and trapping furbearers at Truman Lake ever since it was filled in 1979. For a few years he worked there as a creel census specialist for Missouri Fish & Game.

"All that time on the water taught me that turkeys spend a lot of time loafing along shorelines," Tad says. "I'd see half a dozen flocks somewhere on the shoreline every day. What surprised me was that almost nobody hunts them there. The hunters are all up in the hills. These shoreline turkeys are hardly ever hunted because you need a boat to hunt them, and turkey hunters just don't think of using boats to hunt."

About 8 o'clock the next morning we borrowed a johnboat from Tad's old trapping partner Tom Osenga at Long Shoals Marina and set out to cruise the shoreline.

"You don't need to start too early," Tad explained. "It takes the turkeys about an hour after they come off their roosts to work their way down to the shoreline. If they're not disturbed they'll stay out there.

"Boats don't disturb these turkeys unless you move in on 'em," Tad continued. "They get used to seeing boats go by and hearing human voices all summer. If you stay well offshore and just cruise on by they'll usually stay out in the open."

We had gone only a couple of miles when we spotted a flock of seven or eight turkeys loafing at the wood's edge up ahead.

"Glass 'em," Tad commanded. "Are they gobblers?"

I looked but saw only hens and immatures. As we passed on by, though, Tad said, "I saw a gobbler back in the trees. I saw his beard and his pink head and neck."

He steered the boat in a big U-turn and we headed out of the cove, rounded a long point, and went an equal distance into the cove behind it. Then we tied the boat, put on camo gloves and face masks, loaded our guns, and began the sneak up over the ridge and down to the spot where turkeys were.

"They were under a leaning oak," Tad whispered. "We'll try to spot that tree from well back in the woods and then move toward it. Be very slow. Be quiet."

We moved at a snail's pace, placing every step cautiously and slowly, pressing each advanced foot into the leaves then rolling our weight onto it. It took half an hour to cross the narrow oak-and-hickory ridge, but I knew as we closed on the leaning tree that we'd made no sounds that would spook turkeys. Now we had to get even closer without being seen.

In full camo we picked our way to within 20 yards of the forest edge, stopping and studying the surroundings between each step. Suddenly I saw movement.

I froze. Tad froze at my shoulder.

A hen stepped into the open, head up, alert. Then she darted after a grasshopper, and we knew we had not been marked. A young turkey moved into an opening, then another.

"See the gobbler?" Tad whispered in my ear.

"No," I whispered back.

"I see him. Just to the left of the leaning tree."

"Take him. I can't see him."

Slowly, unnoticeably, Tad raised his gun, then fired.

Turkeys flew in all directions with rushing wings and a chatter of alarm calls, but I still couldn't see what Tad had shot at.

"Did you miss him?" I asked.

"No," Tad scoffed. Then he walked 20 yards to the forest edge and picked up a 17-pound gobbler with an 8-inch beard that he had killed so dead it hadn't even flopped or fluttered.

"You see," he said, "it can be done."

For the next two days, however, our stalks were unsuccessful. Four times we spotted gobbler groups and stalked them. We never knew when we completed a stalk and found no turkeys whether we had been seen or heard, or whether the turkeys had just moved back into the forest on their own volition.

"You made it look pretty easy that first day," I told Tad. "Now it seems impossible."

At 10 o'clock on the fourth morning we spotted a group of six gobblers drinking at the water's edge. We marked the spot carefully and cruised on by, trying to show no interest. They watched us pass, heads up, looking for any sign that we held interest in them.

Once again we got out of their cove, rounded the point, tied the boat, then began a half-mile stalk up over the ridge and down to the spot where we had left the gobblers.

This time a faint breeze gave us some sound cover. Waves lapped the shore and the trees sighed and rattled their leaves. We covered the distance as silently as two men can and crept toward the forest edge certain that we had not spooked the turkeys.

Yet we couldn't see them. I made it all the way to the very edge of the forest—there was only one more oak tree between me and open ground—and still I saw no turkeys.

Had they drifted off? I parted the leaves of a bush that blocked my view and peeked. Nothing. Where had they gone?

I drew back half a step and was ready to gesture Tad to move down next to me when I saw the gobbler.

He was standing perfectly still, sleek and elegant, not 20 yards away, fully in the open but excellently camouflaged. He was looking at me, his head muted in autumn pink and blue, not springtime red. I could not move. Then the gobbler turned sideways, and I saw his long beard bob. As his head went out of sight behind a cluster of leaves I brought the gun to my shoulder, and when the head reappeared I slid the red dot of my Aim-Point sight to the spot where his neck met black feathers. I squeezed off the shot.

Again the air filled with flying turkeys, and I thought for a moment that I had missed. Tad's silence told me he thought so, too.

I yanked up my face mask and stepped into the open, cursing myself for making a mistake I'd made before: I had shot with my head up, not down on the stock where it belongs.

But this time luck was with me. I stepped over a fallen log and nearly put my foot down on my gobbler, which lay dead behind it.

"You miss?" Tad called.

"No," I scoffed, as if I would never do such a thing. "I got him."

Tad rushed down out of the woods, relief showing all over him. "What a bird!" he said, clapping me on the back.

"That's a three- or four-year-old gobbler," he added. He measured the bird's spurs at-1⅛ inches and the beard at 11¼. "When you stalk within 20 yards of a bird like that, you've done it right."

"I was afraid I shot over him," I admitted. "I forgot to get my head down." As it turned out, though, my shot had been saved by the Aim-Point sight, which just happened to be mounted on the gun I had borrowed for this hunt.

"You see, it's not impossible to stalk a mature gobbler in the fall," Tad said. "Just learn to sound like the wind in the trees and move like a shadow. You get good enough at it, you can slip up on anything."

ONE WAY TO CALL FALL GOBBLERS

"Give 'em the sounds of two jakes fighting. When people hear a fight going on they run over to look. Gobblers are no different.

They like to see a good fight, too. Even in the fall," says turkey-hunting guide Rex Suiter of Warsaw, Missouri.

Suiter has called up many fall gobblers by using two push-button calls at once to make the screaming sounds of two jakes fighting.

"It works best if you know where a flock of gobblers roosted," he says. "Go in early the next morning and pick a spot about 100 yards uphill from the roost area. Listen for the birds to fly down. Give them a few minutes on the ground before you start your fighting calls."

Suiter holds a push-button call in each hand and pushes the buttons alternately, one right after the other, for a full minute or more. Then he stops and watches. If he sees nothing moving toward him he repeats the fighting calls for another minute, followed by another one-minute break.

"Gobblers usually feed uphill from their roost in the morning," he says. "If you're located near where they're planning to go anyway there's a good chance they'll run in to watch the fight they hear happening up ahead."

24

THE
EFFECTS OF
WEATHER

"Abnormal weather may have more effects on successful turkey hunting than any other single factor," Jim Clay acknowledges. "But it's hard to make general rules about just how the weather will affect turkey behavior.

"The problem is that what's normal weather to a turkey varies according to where the turkey lives," he adds. "In the hardwood forests of the East, where strong winds are abnormal, high wind puts turkeys in protected hollows and on the backside of windy ridges. But in the West, where strong winds are normal, you see turkeys feeding, breeding, and displaying with their tails to the wind right out in the open, where the wind is so strong that the gobblers' fans are being blown back over their heads.

"When it's raining turkeys avoid tall, wet grass and underbrush.

They either stay on their roosts or stand around in open places, where they can shake the raindrops off and keep their feathers relatively dry. But that does not mean that turkeys can't be hunted successfully on rainy days. They often come to calls on rainy days, but you need to be calling from a place the gobbler can reach without getting himself wet. Plowed field edges, open trails, and old logging roads are good places to set up for turkeys on rainy days.

"The full moon affects turkey behavior a lot," Jim believes. "Most people don't know it, but turkeys will fly down and feed and breed on the ground on bright moonlit nights.

"I once met an old-time turkey poacher who hunted his birds under the light of the full moon. He didn't shoot them off their roost, he called them, and they came to him on the ground. He'd set up around cornfields where the turkeys flew down to feed at night. He

This happy hunter killed his bird on a rainy, windy morning when most folks checked the weather, rolled over, and stayed in bed.

said he liked to hunt them at night because they were less likely to see him move his gun."

Jim says he has shot gobblers that had their crops jammed full of undigested corn at dawn after bright moonlit nights. "You know they didn't hold that corn undigested all night long," he says. "They got down and fed at night."

Night feeding and breeding activity may explain why some hunters find that turkeys respond poorly to calls and stay on their roosts later when the moon is in its full phase. They could be resting after their night's activity.

Jim Clay also notes that gobbling activity increases on a rising or steady barometer and falls off when the barometer is dropping. "I charted gobbling activity for years trying to figure out what influences it," he reports. "That's about all I can say that the data indicated."

Jim's gobbling-activity charts did bring him to one other firm conclusion regarding when and when not to go turkey hunting, however:

"The time to go turkey hunting is whenever you can get to go. The best way to succeed is to be out there trying. There is no one who can tell you how a turkey is going to behave at any certain time. They do what they want to do, and every turkey is different.

"Most hunters look for excuses," Jim declares. "They say it's too windy or too rainy or too cold or too hot, and they stay home. The hunters who get their turkeys every year are in the woods every chance they get, regardless of the weather."

25

HOW YOU CAN HELP TURKEYS IN WINTER

Wild turkey restoration projects have been so successful that turkeys currently populate all of their historical range—and are also spreading into regions where they never lived before.

Now the question is whether turkeys can maintain themselves on their new ranges. In many cases the answer is no—or at least not unless they are given help.

As turkey populations push farther each year into regions only marginally suited for them, they become increasingly dependent on artificial food sources to survive severe winters.

In winter, during deep-snow periods, turkey flocks throughout the northern states commonly gather at dairy farms, where they forage for undigested corn kernels that are scattered when farmers spread manure on top of the snow. When the snow gets too deep for tractor use the turkeys move in close to farm buildings to search for waste corn in manure piles and trench silos.

"If you want to save northern turkey populations, save dairy farms," says Vermont turkey biologist Doug Blodgett.

Trouble is, economic pressures are rapidly shutting down dairy farms in exactly the regions where new wild turkey populations are beginning to thrive and are most dependent on them.

"The future of northern wild turkeys depends on human intervention," says New Hampshire turkey biologist Ted Walski. "When the snow is too deep for turkeys to find sufficient natural wild food, many die unless an artificial food source is provided. In the deep-snow period of 1995 virtually every known flock in New Hampshire was either at a farm feedlot or trench silo, or using backyard bird feeders."

Although state wildlife agencies discourage public deer-feeding programs on the basis that wildlife must live in balance with natural forces in order to remain vigorous, some biologists are making an exception to that rule in the case of the wild turkey, which cannot feed on woody browse like deer or eat emerging treetop buds like grouse.

"If each interested turkey hunter adopted a flock in his town and fed out a few bags of grain during critical deep-snow periods, a substantial turkey population could be maintained," Walski maintains. Wintering turkey flock sites are easy to locate by tracking when snow covers the ground, and by persevering observation.

When deep powder snow limited turkey movement and buried natural food sources in New Hampshire during the early winter of 1995, a network of sportsmen put up posters in general stores and post offices throughout the turkey range offering bags of corn and wheat to people who had turkeys wintering on their properties. Their effort was credited with saving many flocks that would otherwise have perished during the critical deep-snow period.

Throughout the northern turkey range it is becoming common for flocks of wild turkeys to show up at backyard bird feeders when the snow covers up natural forest foods. They follow small birds to the feeding sites and quickly adapt to using them as long as the food supply lasts.

Overcoming their innate wariness to visit bird feeders and other established feeding sites does not seem to have any long-term effects on the turkeys' natural wildness. Experience has shown that as soon as open ground appears and the spring breeding season begins, wild turkeys return to the woods and quickly spread out over the remote countryside.

Some people worry that feeding turkeys concentrates the population and makes it more vulnerable to predation as well as to the spread of disease, but those arguments pale in comparison to the threat of entire flock starvation. If the birds are well fed they are more capable of avoiding predators; well-fed birds are also less prone to disease, particularly during cold weather.

Poor feeding practices can be harmful, however, so the following guidelines should be followed.

- *Do not* feed turkeys within 100 yards of an occupied dwelling, near busy roads, in areas of high visibility, or where dogs run loose.
- *Do not* treat turkeys in ways that might diminish their natural wariness of humans. Keep human contact to a minimum.
- *Do not* become possessive toward turkeys you feed. Wild turkeys are a public resource.
- *Do not* feed turkeys when there is little or no snow cover.
- *Do* feed turkeys cracked or whole-kernel corn, oats, wheat, or nonmedicated commercial turkey rations.
- *Do* feed turkeys regularly by broadcasting feed at a rate of 1 cup per turkey per day. To ensure good distribution among flock

members, scatter feed over a broad area rather than dumping it in mounds.

- *Do* feed turkeys consistently until the flock ceases daily visitation or until severe conditions moderate.

Direct-feeding programs can only help turkeys overcome their immediate needs, however. The unresolved predicament is that most northern regions lack natural winter food sources that are accessible when snow is deep. Natural winter food sources will have to be planted widely before large numbers of northern turkeys will be able to survive extreme winters on their own, particularly where farms are scarce.

It's not that difficult to provide what turkeys need.

Since managing land for turkeys benefits other species of wildlife as well, state wildlife agencies offer management-planning advice and can provide sources for the most beneficial trees, shrubs, and plants.

The National Wild Turkey Federation (P.O. Box 530, Edgefield, SC 29824-0530, 1-800-THE-NWTF) provides free information regarding planting for turkeys according to geographical region. The NWTF also operates a Habitat Enhancement Land Program (HELP) to assist landowners and managers by providing a free catalog of seeds, seedlings, and other helpful products.

"One of the best winter food providers you can plant is Asiatic crab apple," says Ted Walski. "It holds its fruit above the snow all winter and is especially beneficial to turkeys." Other preferred shrubs that bear useful fruit and hold it above the snow all winter are Japanese barberry, European barberry, rugosa rose, bittersweet, hawthorn, highbush cranberry, juniper, winterberry, and sumac.

An excellent new mast-producing tree is the Sweet Hart chestnut—a cross between a blight-resistant Chinese chestnut and a native American chestnut from West Virginia. This species, which is available through the NWTF, usually produces nuts within three years of planting; these small nuts are an excellent mast crop for wildlife and good for human consumption, too.

Woodland managers can assist turkeys by cutting overshadowing trees to "release" wild apple and cherry trees, stimulating fruit production.

Of particular importance to turkeys in winter are forest spring "seeps," where water percolates up from the ground and snow melts first. These seeps can be improved for turkeys by removing any softwoods that overshadow them to allow more sunlight to get in; this will encourage the growth of valuable herbaceous forage such as sedges, grasses, and ferns.

As wild turkeys expand their range northward they are moving into territory that cannot support them naturally in deep-snow winters. Artificial feeding provides temporary relief, but widespread planting of lasting fruits and berries that will remain accessible when snow gets deep is necessary to guarantee the future success of the northern flocks.

Large tracts of open land can be improved for turkey use by planting hedgerows and brushy fencerows of fruiting shrubs and crab apples for winter feed. Plots of standing corn 6 to 12 rows wide and 50 to 100 feet long can be particularly useful to turkeys in winter (although sometimes such plots are stripped by deer before turkeys need them). A food-plot mix that is particularly beneficial to turkeys includes millet, buckwheat, and sunflowers.

Allowing a 50-foot strip of brush to grow along forest edges provides nesting cover, which is often lacking in large, mature forest stands. Planting logging trails and "landings" in grass and legumes, and making small "patch cuts," provides forest openings that turkeys use extensively when their growing poults require abundant grasshoppers and other insects for protein.

"Feeding turkeys is a short-term fix," says Ted Walski. "Planting permanent winter food sources is the key to long-term survival in much of the new range turkeys now occupy."

26

GOURMET
WILD TURKEY

W ild turkey is one of the most delicate of game meats and offers
countless excellent gourmet possibilities—but you can't just
roast it like you would a domestic turkey, or it will be dry.

Do you like veal? Wild turkey is a perfect substitute for it in any
gourmet veal recipe. The faintly pink breast meat even looks like
veal when sliced and laid out on a plate before being cooked. Its delicate flavor is enhanced by being sautéed in a mixture of olive oil
and butter, the way Italians cook many famous veal dishes, and the
process tenderizes the meat and overcomes its natural dryness as
well.

Here are some wild turkey recipes that are guaranteed to please
every palate and make wild turkey a meat to which you will award
the highest regard.

Wild turkey tastes much like farm-raised turkey but it has less fat and is drier. When cooked according to recipes that take this difference into consideration wild turkey becomes one of the very best of gamebird meats.

WILD TURKEY SCALLOPINI

1 turkey breast

3 cups flour

salt and pepper

2 tbsp. olive oil

2 tbsp. butter

½ cup dry white wine

½ cup capers

¼ cup chopped fresh parsley

1 lemon

Slice the turkey breast with the grain in slices 1/2-inch thick. Pound the slices with a meat-tenderizing hammer or the flat side of a meat cleaver until they are ¼-inch thick. Dust with flour, salt, and pepper.

Cover the bottom of a hot skillet with a half-and-half mixture of olive oil and melted butter. Simmer the floured slices of meat until they are golden on both sides (about two minutes per side).

Remove the meat to a serving plate and add wine, capers, and parsley to the pan juices. Squeeze in the juice of one lemon and bring the mixture to a slow boil. Simmer for a minute or two to reduce the sauce to a pleasing consistency, then pour it over the meat and serve.

WILD TURKEY CUTLETS WITH OLIVES

1 boned turkey breast

olive oil

1 finely chopped onion

2 cloves garlic, crushed

1 cup vermouth

1 lemon

1 cup mixed green and black olives

salt and pepper

½ cup chopped fresh parsley

Slice the turkey breast into cutlets ½-inch thick and sauté in olive oil until the meat whitens almost all the way through. Remove the meat to a platter and add more oil to the pan juices. Sauté the onion and garlic until they are translucent. Add the vermouth, cover the pan, and simmer for a minute or two. Then return the turkey to the pan, add the juice of one lemon and the olives, and simmer for five minutes, or until the turkey is tender. Salt and pepper to taste, garnish with chopped parsley, and serve.

WILD TURKEY CORDON BLEU

1 boned turkey breast

1 thin slice ham or prosciutto per serving

1 thin slice Swiss cheese per serving

1 slightly beaten egg

3 tsp. milk

3 tsp. olive oil

2 cups seasoned bread crumbs

Using a long knife, slice the turkey breast with the grain into slices ½-inch thick. Pound the slices with a meat-tenderizing hammer or the flat side of a cleaver until ¼-inch thick.

In a thin coating of olive oil and butter, sauté the meat slices until they whiten. Remove the slices from the skillet and let them drain on a paper towel.

Place one slice of ham or prosciutto and one slice of Swiss cheese on each serving of turkey. Then add one slice of turkey on top.

Holding the layered meat together with your fingers, carefully dip in the mixture of egg, milk, and olive oil, then roll in bread crumbs.

Place on an ovenproof platter and bake at 350°F for about 15 minutes.

GRILLED MARINATED BREAST OF WILD TURKEY

3 cups olive oil
2 cups dry white wine
1 lemon
2 cloves fresh garlic, chopped
salt and pepper
1 turkey breast

With adequate year-round access to nutritious natural foods, mature male wild turkeys commonly grow to more than 20 pounds and provide the basis for a feast fit for a king.

½ cup chopped fresh parsley

½ cup capers

Combine oil, wine, juice of one lemon, garlic, salt, and pepper and stir until thoroughly mixed, then pour into a flat pan.

Using a long knife, slice the turkey breast with the grain into serving-size slices ¾-inch thick. Lay the slices in the pan with the marinade and let marinate for three hours.

Grill on a barbecue until lightly browned. Return the slices briefly to the marinade to moisten, then sprinkle with chopped fresh parsley, capers, and slices of lemon peel.

Serve with linguine and a fresh garden salad.

CAJUN-STYLE BARBECUED WILD TURKEY

1 boned and skinned turkey breast

2 cups chopped chorizo or Italian sausage

2 cups chopped bell peppers

olive oil

salt and pepper

With a sharp long knife, split the turkey breast lengthwise and open it up butterfly-fashion. Cover the butterflied fillet with equal portions of chopped chorizo sausage, or Italian sausage, and chopped bell peppers. Reclose the fillet with the sausage and peppers inside.

Brush the outside of the closed fillet with olive oil and sprinkle with salt and pepper. Place on a barbecue and cook until lightly browned and tender, basting occasionally with oil.

When done, slice ½-inch thick across the grain and serve.

WILD TURKEY SAUSAGE WITH SAGE AND APPLE

1 small onion, chopped fine

1 clove garlic, chopped fine

¼ cup olive oil

1 cup dry white wine

1 lb. turkey leg meat

2 large apples, chopped fine

¼ cup chopped parsley

2 tsp. ground sage

1 tbsp. kosher salt

½ tsp. coarse black pepper

3 ft. sausage casings, soaked 30 minutes in warm water

Sauté the onion and garlic in olive oil until they are limp. Add the white wine and simmer four to five minutes.

Boil the turkey leg meat until done, then cut into chunks and grind with a medium grinder blade. In a large bowl, thoroughly mix the ground turkey meat with the sautéed vegetables and the remaining ingredients. Sauté a small patty of this mixture in a skillet until browned and taste to see if the seasoning suits your palate. Adjust if necessary.

Using a sausage stuffer or funnel, force the mixture into the casings and twist off every 3 inches until the mixture is used up.

To cook: Simmer in water for 15 minutes or sauté in an oiled skillet until lightly browned.

SOUTHERN-FRIED WILD TURKEY

1 boned and skinned turkey breast and 2 thighs

2 cups milk

2 cups flour

salt and pepper

Cajun spice mixture

1 qt. peanut oil

I'm supposed to avoid fried food and probably you are, too, but southern-fried wild turkey tastes so good that I occasionally succumb to its temptation—and always leave the table wishing I could eat it more often. It's great!

Cut the skinned wild turkey breast meat into cubes about 1-1/2 inches square. Dip the cubes, along with the turkey thighs, into milk, then roll them in a mixture of flour, salt, pepper, and your favorite brand of Cajun spices (Tony Cachere's is my choice). Deep-fry until golden in peanut oil at 375°F.

Serve with coleslaw, turnip greens boiled with ham, and baked beans.

TURKEY SALAD

4 cups cooked (boiled and boned), ½-inch cubes of turkey meat
2 tsp. grated onion
1 cup sliced celery
1 cup chopped fresh apple
1 cup mayonnaise
2 tbsp. cider vinegar
salt
¼ tsp. freshly ground pepper
1 head washed leaf lettuce

Put the turkey, onion, celery, and apple in a bowl. Add the mayonnaise, vinegar, salt, and pepper and blend thoroughly. Chill, then spoon onto a bed of chilled lettuce leaves.

TURKEY CROQUETTES

1 lb. cooked and ground turkey leg meat
½ tsp. salt
¼ cup chopped celery (with leaves)
large pinch cayenne pepper
½ cup chopped green pepper
½ cup chopped onion
1 cup thick white sauce (butter, milk, and flour), plus extra for serving
2 eggs, lightly beaten

2 cups bread crumbs

canola oil

This recipe is a good way to use turkey legs.

Boil the legs until they are cooked thoroughly, then separate the meat from the bones. Skin and grind the meat using a coarse blade.

Mix the ground turkey with salt, celery, cayenne pepper, green pepper, onion, and white sauce until it's fully blended. Cover with foil and refrigerate until chilled. Then form into cone-shaped patties. Dip the patties in the beaten egg, roll them in bread crumbs and set aside. Pour 1 inch of canola oil into a large skillet and bring to medium heat. Add the croquettes and cook until browned on all sides. Put them on a platter and cover with more white sauce.

27

ONE LAST
DECOY TRICK

In the spring of 1997 I embarked on a turkey-hunting odyssey. I left my home in frozen New Hampshire in mid-March and headed south, following the turkey woods down the Appalachian Mountain chain all the way to Georgia, then pushed on to central Florida to open my turkey-hunting season in prime southern Osceola turkey swampland.

After an enlightening Florida hunt I swung back up to the Georgia mountains and hunted Eastern turkeys in the high country, then headed west to Arkansas to hunt Easterns again in the flat piney woods. I hunted Rio Grandes in the ranchlands of the Texas panhandle and pushed north into Nebraska to hunt Merriams in the Pine Ridge country. Turning east, I barreled on to northern Missouri for another Eastern turkey hunt in rolling hardwood timber, then moved on to Virginia for one more Eastern turkey hunt before pointing the truck north and heading home to New Hampshire—where turkey season was just about to open.

I was on the road for seven weeks and at the end of it, 8,000 miles later, rather than having had my fill of turkey hunting I was more cranked up than ever.

My truck, however, had had enough.

Before leaving on the trip I had considered trading it in for a new pickup but decided against it. Why put all that mileage on a new vehicle? My dealer assured me that a few thousand more miles on the old truck wouldn't seriously affect the trade-in price—and furthermore, I liked the old truck. We'd been to a lot of good places together, and I thought a turkey-hunting odyssey was in keeping with the way the old Ford was used to being treated.

We were getting sick of each other by the time we struggled back to New Hampshire, however. The time to trade had come.

My local Ford dealer is a turkey hunter himself, and he couldn't wait to hear about my trip. What impressed him most were my accounts of how decoys were used to make gobblers take those last few steps that brought them into close killing range. He could hardly believe I'd killed nine gobblers over decoys, most of them at less than 20 yards when they went head to head with the little standing jake decoy.

"I've got to get a set of decoys," he said. "I never tried them."

Then we talked trucks.

"I've got two trucks here for you," he told me. "I ordered them in just for you. Both green—I know you like a green truck. One stick shift and one automatic—you can take your choice."

We got down to the nitty-gritty and talked deals. We got close, but in the end $400 still separated us. I said I wouldn't budge. My old truck probably still had another 100,000 miles in it. He said I might be right, but then you never know what repairs will cost along the way.

So we talked turkey hunting some more. I told him how he should set his jake decoy where it'll be most comfortable to shoot and no more than 20 yards away and how, if a gobbler comes in at all, that's where he'll go every time. I said I like to put my hen decoy up on a stump when I can, to make it more visible from a distance. I told him about a big old bird I shot one time at 7 yards when he came in almost on top of me and so intent on the jake decoy that he never saw me raise my gun.

"I've just got to get a set of those decoys," he said. "I never tried 'em."

"The ones I use are so realistic you have be careful not to shoot the decoy by mistake," I explained. "They stand on a spindle and even the faintest breath of air makes them move like real birds."

"Boy, I'd like to see that."

"I've got a pair right in the truck," I announced. "I'll get 'em out and show 'em to you."

Man, did he like those decoys. He held them up in the light and turned them this way and that. He rolled them up and realized how easy they'd be to carry in his vest pocket. He noticed the four pellet holes in the jake decoy's head that got there when I shot a big old gobbler that was head to head with it.

"I've just got to get a set of these," he said. "I wish I had 'em right now. I'm going hunting in the morning."

Of course, I knew I had him then.

"They're yours," I said. "Just drop that last $400 off the price of that truck and they're yours."

He winced like he'd been slapped. But then he looked over his shoulder to make sure no one was around.

"Okay," he said. "You've got a deal. But don't tell any of my salesmen about this because I don't let 'em take anything in trade but cash and vehicles. If they knew I'd taken these decoys, I'd never live it down."

So we went back inside and started filling out papers. The dealer put the decoys behind his desk, out of sight. Eventually the deal was done. We were shaking hands when suddenly his sales manager came across the room and went around behind the dealer's desk to get a form out of a drawer.

The manager had to move the decoys out of the way. He looked at them for a long time, and then he looked at me and his eyes narrowed.

He picked up the jake decoy and admired it.

"Hmmmph," he said. "I guess I won't ask how much these decoys cost the company."

INDEX

diaphragm mouth calls, 42, 43, 46,
    48–49, 59, 92–93, 124, 155
dog whistles, 88
double-reed calls, 48
droppings, as sign, 65, 124
drumming, 37–38
Drury, Marc, 42–43, 77–78, 80,
    85–88, 89, 128

early-morning hunting, 46, 91–92
Eastern subspecies, 2, 37, 43, 61,
    151, 199–200
"either-sex" hunting season, 58
Emberson, Mike, 35

Feather-Flex decoys, 11, 14, 21, 27, 31
    safety decoys, 33–34
feathers, as sign, 65
fiber wadding, 148, 149
Field & Stream magazine, 1
floating caller, 81–84, **82**
flocks, 66–67, 173–74
fly-down calls, 46, 71, 118
Foy, Ronnie, 9–11, 20, 21, 22, 27
friction calls, 47–48, 52, 53, **54,**
    55–56, 75, 87
full-strut decoys, 15, **16,** 30
furniture, as material for turkey
    calls, 53

Gilled Marinated Breast of Wild
    Turkey (recipe), 193–94
gobblers, **4,** 8, 175–77, **193.** *See
    also* jakes; longbeards
    decoys and, 11, 13–20, 99, 101–2,
        104, 108, 119, 166–67
    dominant, 15, 18, 19–20, 26, 30,
        31, 36, **125,** 126, 160

"henned-up," **86,** 93–94, 117
    instinctive wariness of, 106, 139
    lonely, 85, **86,** 87–88
    mating display behavior, 26,
        28–31, **29,** 66, 139, 140, 160
    movement patterns of, 97–104
    nonbreeding, 123–26, **124, 125,**
        160
    response to hen calls, 42–50,
        71–75, 88, 106–9, 126, 160
    roosting habits, 75–76
    silence of, 62–67, 117–22, **120,**
        122
    subdominant, 18–19, 26, 36
    use of floating caller for stub-
        born birds, 81–84, **82**
Gobblin' Thunder turkey chokes,
    141, **141**
guides, 1, 44, 93, 98, 178
gunsmiths, 137, 147

Habitat Enhancement Land
    Program (HELP), 186
half-strut decoys, 15, **16,** 30
hats, shooting performance and,
    134
Hauer, John, 153, 155–60
head shots, 131, 139, 143, 144, 148,
    168
hens, 13–14, 75–76, 85, 112, 166
    breeding behavior of, 91, 94
    clucking sounds of, 41, 42
    competition among, 25–26
    cutting sounds of, 70–71
    dominant, 47
    dominant gobblers and, 30
    in flocks, 66–67, 99
    incubating eggs, 126, 160